ALONG
the ROAD

ALONG
the ROAD

HOW JESUS USED GEOGRAPHY
TO TELL GOD'S STORY

JOHN A. BECK

Discovery House®
from Our Daily Bread Ministries

Discovery House is affiliated with Our Daily Bread
Ministries, Grand Rapids, Michigan.

Requests for permission to quote from this book should be directed to:
Permissions Department, Discovery House, P.O. Box 3566,
Grand Rapids, MI 49501, or contact us by
email at permissionsdept@dhp.org.

Interior design by Sherri L. Hoffman

Library of Congress Cataloging-in-Publication Data

Names: Beck, John A., 1956- author.
Title: Along the road : how Jesus used geography to tell God's story
    / Dr. John A. Beck.
Description: Grand Rapids : Discovery House, 2018.
Identifiers: LCCN 2017049759 | ISBN 978-1-62707-732-3 (pbk.)
Subjects: LCSH: Jesus Christ—Travel. | Travel in the Bible. |
    Bible—Geography. | Israel—Description and travel. | Bible stories.
Classification: LCC BT303.9 .B43 2018 | DDC 220.9/1—dc23
LC record available at https://lccn.loc.gov/2017049759

Printed in the United States of America

First printing in 2018

For Anne Marie Beck, Eula Beck, and Miles Beck,
our three grandchildren who recently joined our family
and the Kingdom of God

CONTENTS

INTRODUCTION

"Come, follow me" (Matthew 4:19). With these words, Jesus invited Peter and Andrew to join him on a lifelong walk. And when Jesus said "walk," he literally meant *walk*. Most of Jesus's teaching was done outdoors as he walked along the road. He led his listeners to specific locations, then knit his lessons into the soil and scenery.

At times, Jesus simply took advantage of what was in view: he spoke about a city on a hill, farmers in the fields, and birds of the air. But on other walks, there is more to a location than what lies on the surface.

Jesus gives us the same invitation he offered to Peter and Andrew. "Come, follow me on a walk along the road so I can tell you more of God's story." When we walk to those places—whether in actuality or as readers of God's Word—we may experience what I call geographic déjà vu, the feeling that we have been in these places before.

That is exactly why Jesus brings us to places like this. He is inviting us to revisit the backstory, the memories contained in these locations, so he can build a new lesson on them. This book is about places like that.

We Are Organizers

When we consider how we organize and study the contents of our Bible, we will more easily see this relationship between places, what happened here before, and what we can learn from them today. It goes without saying (though it won't here) that each of us is an organizer. We organize the cookware in our kitchens. We organize the clothing in our closets. We organize the tools in our workshops. We organize, in part, because there are things that naturally belong together. Although no two people, not even

9

those living in the same house, organize their stuff in the precisely the same way, all of us organize by putting together things that belong together.

Ways We Organize Our Bible

We not only organize the things we own, we also organize the contents of our Bible. Now, it is true that all the pages of our Bible belong together because they all come from the mind of our one God. But some Bible passages read most naturally in the company of others. So we organize our Bible reading.

Let's consider three ways in which we do this. First, we can organize the contents of our Bible against the passage of time—that is, chronologically. Some stories occur at or near the same time; others occur centuries apart. When we organize the Bible chronologically, we bring books and Bible passages together that share a similar moment in history.

For example, it is natural for us to read Ezra and Nehemiah together because they discuss the era immediately following the return of Israel from its exile in Babylon. We will find it helpful to read Lamentations, which grieves the destruction of Jerusalem, together with the description of that event in 2 Kings 25 and 2 Chronicles 36. And we will benefit from reading the New Testament epistles with an ear tuned to the story of the early church in Acts. In all these cases, we are organizing the Bible's content chronologically.

We can also organize the contents of our Bible topically—that is, in theological categories. The Holy Spirit often inspired Bible authors to write about similar topics, in whatever era they lived. These topics form theological categories, and the dimension of Christian scholarship that studies the Bible in this way is called "systematic theology." It gathers passages under headings like creation, sin, Christ, salvation, the church, and the last things.

Ironically, when we buy a bound Bible from the bookstore, its contents have already been organized for us. But realize that when the books of the Bible were written, they were produced one at a time and existed as separate documents; the Genesis-to-Revelation ordering that is familiar to us was *not* part of the process of divine inspiration.

It was not until about AD 100 that Christians began using the codex (a book with a binding) for gathering their sacred writings. The codex required that the sixty-six books be assembled in a certain order and, for better or worse, the order of the books can create in our minds either a closer or a more distant relationship between their content.

Organizing Our Bible Geographically

But what about organizing the contents of the Bible geographically, and experiencing God's story as Jesus told it while walking along the road? This method brings together Bible stories, poetry, and letters that share a common locale even if they do not occur at the same time in history—even if they are many pages apart in our Bibles. Let me give you a quick example.

Two stories, from the lives of Elisha and Jesus, share a common setting (2 Kings 4:8–37 and Luke 7:11–17). These stories are separated by nearly 850 years and by some 1,425 pages in my Bible. They don't even share an obvious geographical link, because the first is set in the village of Shunem and the second in Nain. But when we look closely at the geography, we see that both events occur on the same isolated mountain in the Jezreel Valley. These two villages are on opposite sides of the same ridge of Mount Moreh, just a little over a mile apart. While history puts centuries between them, geography separates them by less than twenty-five minutes' walk.

If we are organizing our Bibles geographically, we ask a new set of questions. Why did Jesus perform a miracle in this location? How was the reaction of those who witnessed the miracle conditioned by what had happened here in Elisha's day? What can I learn by studying these two Bible stories together?

The purpose of this study is to help you read the Bible like a walker, to organize the contents of your Bible geographically. This is not at the expense of studying the Bible chronologically or in theological categories; it is just another way to consider the relationship between verses.

As you begin paying attention to *where* things happened in the Bible, you will get the feeling you have been in a place before. This is what I call geographic déjà vu. It is the signal that we've found stories we should study together.

Overview of the Book

In the next chapter, I will further explain the idea of organizing your Bible like a walker. I will tell you how I happened on this idea, and why it has a deep and enduring connection to those who first experienced the contents of our Bible by walking the Promised Land.

After that, each of the five parts of this book will showcase a type of lesson Jesus taught by taking us to places we've been before. In Part One, "Jesus, Geography, and Old Testament Prophecy," we walk with Jesus to places mentioned in Old Testament prophecies about the coming Messiah. Jesus visited those spots to confirm he *is* the promised Messiah.

In Part Two, "Jesus, Geography, and Substitution," we walk with Jesus to places that the Israelites had walked in Old Testament times. Jesus went to those places to replicate the experiences of Israel, showing he was fully human but able to succeed where mortals failed. These places teach that Jesus saves us from our sin by being our Substitute.

In Part Three, "Jesus, Geography, and Pagan Land Claims," we walk with Jesus to places where the evil one found success in the Old Testament. In each case, Jesus goes to these places to deliver a stunning defeat to Satan.

In Part Four, "Jesus, Geography, and Divine Titles," we walk with Jesus to locations associated with Old Testament titles like

Messiah, prophet, king, and judge. Jesus visited these places to link himself to those titles and help us better understand his roles in our lives.

Finally in Part Five, "Jesus, Geography, and Our Mission," Jesus walks us to places we have been before *with him*. He takes us back to these places to confirm or expand upon a message that he had delivered there during an earlier visit.

"Come, follow me," Jesus says. It is time for us to lace up our walking shoes and get underway.

1

ORGANIZING THE BIBLE LIKE A WALKER

WHETHER I AM BACKPACKING WILDERNESS trails of the American West or strolling the streets of our hometown after dinner with my wife, I love to walk. That carries over into my professional life as a Bible teacher in Israel.

I walk ancient roads with my students, discussing the geography of the Promised Land and the Bible verses that connect to it. This is how I started organizing my Bible geographically, and it is a story I will tell in this chapter.

But I also want to show that this idea—of organizing the Bible while walking along the road—did not start with me. It has roots reaching deeply into the way people have always "read their Bible" in the Promised Land. This chapter will tell that story too.

Finally, I want you to know that even if you cannot join me for a walk in Israel, you can walk along the road with Jesus, organizing your Bible geographically, without leaving the comforts of your home. This chapter will help you get started.

My Walks in the Promised Land

Let me start with my story. I am a professor at Jerusalem University College in Israel. I meet Bible readers from around the world, people who have come to Israel to learn about the geography of this special land. While I spend a short time discussing geography in a classroom, most of the course is taught outdoors. And by design, we learn the land by walking the land.

Over two weeks—hour after hour, day after day, one foot ahead of the other—we walk more than one hundred miles. We walk in sunshine, under cloudy skies, in the rain, and even in the rare snow storm! We move from one geographical setting to the next and from one ecosystem to another, collecting impressions of this land that the Lord called his own.

During the course of a day, I pick out specific locations to stop, not only so we can rest but because the view captures the unique qualities of the subregion we are studying that day. I speak about geology, topography, water resources, climate, plants, and animals. I discuss how each place shaped the lives of the people who lived there, what I call its "human geography." We talk about how these people got water, the food they grew, how they built their homes, and how they traveled in this segment of the land. And before we move on to the next teaching location, we enjoy a conversation about the key Bible stories and passages linked to the place.

After years of doing this, I realized that I was organizing my Bible geographically. Think about that for a moment: as I take my students to a certain location, I am often in a place that hosted more than one event or element of biblical communication. Take Shechem as an example. There are significant stories that occurred here at the times of Abraham, Jacob, Joshua, Rehoboam, and Jesus. If I were teaching the course chronologically, I would have to return to Shechem five times! I think you can see the problem with that way of organizing the course. So instead, I teach all five stories on the same visit.

This way of thinking about the Bible created connections between stories and passages that in my previous study had long lived apart. I began to connect stories like Israel's extended stay in the wilderness with Jesus's temptation in the wilderness; Solomon's coronation as king in the Kidron Valley with Jesus's Palm Sunday entry into Jerusalem; and Jesus's Sermon on the Mount with the Great Commission. You see, it didn't matter where those passages resided on the timeline or how many pages separated them in my Bible—if the land brought them together, so did I. And that became the fertile soil in which new insights grew, insights I will share in the remaining chapters of this book.

My love for the outdoors, for walking, and for teaching the Bible joined forces to give me a new tool for Bible study. I was organizing my Bible like a walker.

Ancient Walks in the Promised Land

The idea of organizing the Bible while walking along the road is particularly the story of those who walked this land in Bible times. To better understand that, we need to consider how their travel experiences and their Bible reading differ from our own.

People then walked everywhere. While I walk to exercise or relax, people in Bible times walked out of necessity. They did not have cars, trains, or even bicycles; donkeys and camels were available, but used more as pack animals than for transporting people. So with rare exception, people traveling from place to place in Bible times did so by foot.

When a severe famine imperiled the Promised Land, Jacob walked to Egypt. When there was a festival in Jerusalem, believers walked to the holy city. When there was an extended family wedding in Cana, Jesus and the disciples walked there from Nazareth. And when Paul took the good news about Jesus from Iconium to Lystra, he walked. Walking was simply how you got where you needed to go.

I like to walk alone, sometimes over long distances. But solo travel was never advisable for those living in Bible times, because walking for them was filled with dangers I don't have to face. Read Psalm 121, a travel psalm, and you begin to get a sense for that. Their risks included falls on steep terrain, injury during robbery, being swept away by a flooding river, and the ever-present possibility of attack by large predators. People in Bible times typically traveled in the company of others to minimize the risks they faced when walking.

As these people walked in groups, they passed the time by talking with one another. Certainly, there were times when the only sound heard was the scuffing of sandals on the dirt path. But more typically, traveling time was passed in conversation, talks that ranged across the horizon of human experience just as ours do. People would have spoken about funny things the kids had done, the failing health of a family member, even the weather they expected to encounter the next day. But walking also provided time to reflect on and talk about the more important questions of life: Who is God? How does he think about human beings? What does he expect of us?

Today, what we think about such matters is largely guided by a Book that was not available to them in the way it is to us. Even though the first books of the Bible were put into writing as early as the fifteenth century before Christ, few copies existed. The printing press was not invented until the fifteenth century after Christ. The first photocopier did not reach the market until 1959. In Bible times, those fortunate enough to own a portion of God's Word had a document that had been copied by hand. As you can imagine, this made any written document rare and very expensive. The king of Israel stood out in that he had his own copy of God's Word (Deuteronomy 17:18)—the average person did not.

Another complication, as if one were needed, is associated with literacy. Reading skills as we know them today were not a feature of the ancient world. Ancient evidence indicates that average workers may have had a lower level of functional literacy. But the higher skills required for more complex reading tasks, like those required to understand Scripture, were enjoyed by at most only 10 percent of those in Bible times.

Walking, Organizing, and Teaching the Bible in Bible Times

Despite these obstacles, people living in this era were not without a "Bible." They learned and reflected on what God said while walking the land of the Bible. When they hiked through their homeland, they did not just see rivers, mountains, and wilderness—they saw biblical events, directions God had given, and promises the Lord had made, all of which were intimately linked to the land.

When Old Testament believers walked past Shechem, they thought about the Lord appearing to Abram in that location, making a set of promises that linked the land of Canaan with the patriarch's family and the promise to redeem the world from sin (Genesis 12:1–7). When they walked past Mount Tabor, they recalled the story of Deborah and Barak as the Lord provided unexpected victory over the Canaanites, with their iron chariots (Judges 4–5). When believers walked past Bethlehem, they thought of Micah's prophecy that promised this town would be the birthplace of the long-awaited Messiah (5:2).

People of Bible times may not have had the written Bible that we do (or even the skill to read one), but they navigated a place filled with Bible content. For them, walking the land was the equivalent of our reading the Bible.

And they were organizing the content of God's revelation geographically. They linked God's first appearance to Abram in the Promised Land (Genesis 12:6–7) and the services of rededication which Joshua held for Israel seven centuries later (Joshua 8:30–35; 24:1–28)—because they shared a common location in the valley between Mount Gerizim and Mount Ebal near ancient Shechem. They linked the story of Gideon's great victory over the invading eastern peoples (Judges 7:1–22) and Saul's great defeat at the hands of the Philistines (1 Samuel 31)—both stories are based near springs which are just a little over a mile apart at the base of Mount Gilboa. They connected two attempts of Satan to derail the ministry of Jesus at Mount Hermon—here Satan tempted Jesus to abandon his mission, both at the start of his earthly ministry (Matthew 4:8–11) and again as he made the final turn to Jerusalem (Matthew 16:22–23).

This notion of engaging and teaching God's thoughts by walking the land is mentioned by Moses. The book of Deuteronomy summarizes God's teachings for Israel as the people prepare to enter the Promised Land, and Moses told parents to teach these things to their children. Notice where that instruction is to occur: "Teach them to your children, talking about them when you sit at home, *and when you walk along the road*, when you lie down and when you get up" (Deuteronomy 11:19, emphasis mine).

Parents spent time with their children walking to family functions or to festivals in Jerusalem. This walking time was teaching time, and the land was the textbook that suggested topics for discussion.

We do something similar when we take our children to places with deep roots in our own history. A drive through Washington, DC, my national capital, is a good example of this. In one afternoon, we can teach our children about the assassination of President Abraham Lincoln and the famous "I Have a Dream" speech of Martin Luther King Jr. Layers of history build vertically on one location, and we can pick one event from the column to study it in isolation from the others, or we can compare and contrast events brought together in this place. We can also explore the influence of one event on subsequent events that occurred here. This is exactly what Moses urged parents to do as they walked the land with their sons and daughters.

So what I do with my students in Israel really isn't unique—it has very deep roots in the history of God's people in the Promised Land. As they walked, they engaged the thoughts and promises of God that were linked to places. They organized the revelation of God geographically, learning and teaching lessons from the land.

Reading Our Bible like a Walker

Now I invite you to do the same thing, to think how your reading and study might change if you organized the contents of the Bible geographically. That is, you read it like a walker would.

You do not need to be on a study program with me in Israel. You don't even need to be walking. You can read and organize your Bible like a walker even if you're sitting in your home.

This will, however, take an adjustment to your usual mode of thinking about the Bible. Most of us, and I include myself in this statement, were never taught to read our Bibles this way. We have organized our Bible readings chronologically and thematically, but not geographically. It will take some effort on our part to make the change. So as this chapter concludes, let me suggest a plan for adding this new form of Bible study to the helpful things you already do.

First, acknowledge that all Bible stories (and most other forms of Bible communication) have a physical setting that aids in our comprehension. Yet for many western Bible readers who have not been to the Holy Land, the content floats above the land rather than interacting with it intimately. If that describes you, the first step is acknowledging the intentional grounding of the Bible's message in place.

Second, actively look for clues within a Bible passage that indicate *where* the events or teaching occur. Even if you are in the habit of reading past them, I can assure you that the clues are there. This step calls for us to slow our reading down, to be intentional about seeking the clues. They may be the name of a city or region, the mention of a geographic feature (such as "a high mountain"), or the signal of a specific ecosystem like the wilderness.

Third, look for other stories or elements of Bible communication that share these spaces. This will take some work, as you use your experience with the Bible, your concordance, and an atlas to create a list of passages that belong in the same geographical context. When you begin to organize the Bible in this way, you'll discover that there are Jerusalem stories, wilderness stories, and Caesarea Maritima stories—they share settings and deserve to be read and interpreted together.

Now it's time to unleash your creative, spiritual energy on the list. Your goal is to see if and how those stories or passages, all sharing a physical setting, might interact with one another to enhance our understanding of God's communication with us. Here are some questions that can help you toward that end:

- Other than place, what do the passages have in common? Think in terms of people, events, and the words and phrases that make up the text. In the stories of Gideon and Saul at the base of Mount Gilboa, we have different people of different eras, facing the same experience—an overwhelming military invasion—in the same place.

- Do the passages that share a place also share a theme? In the case of Gideon and Saul again, the stories revolve around the faith (or lack of faith) shown by a leader in the face of a military invasion.

- Do the geographically linked passages of the Bible build on one another, teaching a lesson God wants us to learn? The lesson could be taught by repeating and reinforcing, by way of contrast, or by supporting or defeating an expectation. For example, Shechem was a powerful center of worship in the Old Testament, a place to think and speak carefully about the revelation of God. It makes sense that Solomon's son, Rehoboam, would go there for his coronation, but we are struck by how secularized the process sounds, completely out of step with what we would expect at this sacred site.

This chapter has been long on background and short on Bible study. That will change as we begin to look more closely at stories from Jesus's life. But before you turn to the next chapter, I invite you to anchor this idea of reading the Bible like a walker more firmly in place, by considering the questions that follow.

———— Questions for Reflection and Discussion ————

1. How much do you enjoy walking? What do you think about when you walk?

2. During your Bible reading and study time, in which way (or ways) do you typically organize the content? In your own words, explain the phrase "organizing your Bible like a walker."

3. In which Bible story or stories have you seen geography playing an important role?

4. For practice, read Luke 10:38–42 and John 11:17–44, two stories linked geographically to Bethany, and answer the following questions:

    • Other than geography, what do the two passages have in common?

    • Do these stories share a common theme?

    • How does reading these stories together change the way you understand them?

PART ONE

Jesus, Geography, and
Old Testament Prophecy

GOD'S STORY PERMEATES THE SOIL and scenery of the Promised Land. To walk this land is to meet this story.

But walking the land with Jesus takes us a step farther. In the walks featured in this part of the book, we will see how they connect Jesus geographically to the promises made by the Old Testament prophets. Men like Isaiah, Micah, and Zechariah put places like Bethlehem, Nazareth, Capernaum, and Bethphage on our map. Jesus takes us to these same locations to build on those lessons—and fulfill those promises. In doing so, he confirms that he is the Messiah, the promised Savior from sin.

This is no small matter. In our own way, each of us has failed to live up to God the Father's high standards. Each of us deserves to be punished for our sins, and that imposes a burden that weighs heavily on our souls. We crave the deep and abiding spiritual peace that comes only when we know we have a Savior, and that is what makes these walks with Jesus so worthwhile. When we walk along the road to places the prophets mentioned, Jesus confirms that he is our Savior from sin.

N
W
E
S
MEDITERRANEAN SEA
GALILEE
Capernaum
Sea of Galilee
Sepphoris
Nazareth
Caesarea Maritima
Ginae
SAMARIA
Sychar
Joppa
RIDGE ROUTE
Ramah
Jerusalem
Bethlehem
Herodium
JUDEA
0
10 mi
0
15 km
Mary and Joseph to Bethlehem

2

WALKING WITH JESUS FROM
NAZARETH TO BETHLEHEM

THE FIRST WALK WE'LL TAKE with Jesus occurs before Jesus can walk. It is the hike with Mary, Joseph, and the soon-to-be-born Jesus from Nazareth to Bethlehem.

This story is among the best known in the Bible. Mary, the expectant mom, and Joseph, her husband, lived in Nazareth. God sent special messengers to each one to tell them that they were going to have a son (Matthew 1:18–25; Luke 1:26–38). What is more, the child would be conceived miraculously, setting their boy apart from all the other children in Nazareth. This baby boy was the long-awaited Savior from sin.

As Mary's due date approached, tax matters took this couple to Bethlehem, about seventy miles to the south. Rome had ordered a census be taken to improve their records and revenue collection. "So Joseph also went up from the town of Nazareth in Galilee to Judea, to Bethlehem the town of David, because he belonged to the house and line of David. He went there to register with Mary, who was pledged to be married to him and was expecting a child" (Luke 2:4–5).

While they were in Bethlehem, Mary gave birth to Jesus in a shelter for animals, placing her newborn in a feedbox. Soon after, the evening sky near Bethlehem brightened as the Lord's angels announced the birth to shepherds tending their flocks. These Christmas angels filled the air with praise and urged the shepherds to go into Bethlehem for "today in the town of David a Savior has been born to you; he is the Messiah, the Lord" (Luke 2:11). The shepherds ran to the shelter to confirm the angels' report and then shared the news with others.

What kind of place was the town of Bethlehem? A very different place than the city we visit today. Bethlehem in Jesus's day counted its residents in the hundreds, while today's Bethlehem is inhabited by tens of thousands. When Mary and Joseph walked to Bethlehem, the locals grew grain and raised livestock; today it is more likely that someone living in Bethlehem works in one of the many shops, restaurants, and hotels used by tourists. The simple, unadorned cave that served as the animal shelter where Jesus was born now resides under the ornately decorated Church of the Nativity.

Many things have changed in Bethlehem but the land beneath the buildings has not. The New Testament town clung to the central watershed ridge, leaving the basin below as a place to grow winter wheat and pasture sheep and goats during the summer months. Although Bethlehem was a mere five miles from Jerusalem, it was more rural and less crowded, with a less sophisticated feel.

As we walk into Bethlehem with Mary and Joseph, we get the overwhelming feeling that we have been in this place before. And we *have* been here before, because Bethlehem provides the setting for two Old Testament stories.

First, it is the backdrop for most of the account of Ruth and Naomi, two widows struggling to make ends meet. Bethlehem was Naomi's hometown and Ruth's adopted home (Ruth 1:1, 22), the place of a heartwarming story that moves the women from poverty to plenty, thanks to the God-arranged romance between Ruth and Boaz. Most importantly, it is a place in which the Lord demonstrated both his willingness and his ability to provide a solution for a family in harm's way.

Turn a few more pages in your Bible and you will come to the next significant Bethlehem story. This time it was the nation of Israel that had a problem in need of a solution. Its first king, Saul, had failed to be the leader the Lord wanted him to be. Saul's failings degraded both the physical and spiritual well-being of those in his kingdom, so Israel needed a new leader, a better leader, a leader after the Lord's own heart. We find ourselves walking toward Bethlehem with Samuel, searching for a solution for Israel as a whole (1 Samuel 16:1).

This is where our two stories meet geographically. The Lord sent Samuel to the family of Jesse, the grandson of Boaz and Ruth. Samuel interviewed seven sons in the family but found none of them to be the Lord's choice. We feel a hint of frustration in the question he asks Jesse: "Are these all the sons you have?" (1 Samuel 16:11).

The youngest of the brothers, David, was tending the sheep in the fields near Bethlehem. Once this young man stood before Samuel, the Lord made it clear that David was his choice—and Samuel anointed him as Israel's next king. Just as Bethlehem provided Naomi's family with a solution in a time of financial crisis, so it offered the nation of Israel a solution to its leadership crisis.

But Bethlehem had one more solution to offer, one that would benefit the entire world. We first hear about it from Micah, a prophet who lived about seven hundred years before the birth of Jesus. Once again, very poor leadership had landed Israel in crisis.

On more than one occasion, the empire of Assyria invaded the Promised Land. This was no accident of history—the Lord allowed these invasions as a call to Israel to repent. Micah's voice summoned God's people to see the world as the Lord did.

Micah aimed sharp criticism at kings, prophets, priests, and judges, all of whom had failed in their assignments (Micah 3). He urged the people to see the invasions as a spiritual wakeup call, and for those who listened, he offered a word of encouragement. A new era would dawn, Micah said, one dominated by peace under the leadership of a divine King. Other prophets had spoken about this age and this leader, but Micah adds one more incredible detail by providing the coordinates for the Messiah's birth: "But you, Bethlehem Ephrathah, though you are small among the clans of Judah, out of you will come for me one who will be ruler over Israel, whose origins are from of old, from ancient times" (5:2).

The level of precision here is remarkable. Micah identifies the tribal territory, Judah. He names the town, Bethlehem. And he even gives the alternate Old Testament name of the town, Ephrathah. In the ancient world, this is about as precise a plotting as you can give. Micah uses it to mark the very spot in which the Messiah would be born. The descendant promised to King David, the one who would rule an eternal kingdom, could now be born in just one place—David's hometown of Bethlehem.

When we walk with Mary and Joseph to Bethlehem for Jesus's birth, we are going to a place we have been before. And the gospel writers are insistent that we think about where we are on this walk. Consider this: there are many details of this trip to Bethlehem that Matthew and Luke have not included in their accounts, but they are adamant that we get the geography correct.

In telling the story of Jesus's early life, Matthew and Luke don't just mention Bethlehem (or its alternative label in Luke's gospel, "town of David") once or twice. Read Matthew 2 and Luke 2 and you will find that Bethlehem is mentioned *nine* times! Why do these writers want to be sure that we see the account of Jesus's birth as a Bethlehem story?

Matthew and Luke use our previous visits to Bethlehem (from our reading of the Old Testament) to shape our reaction to the birth of Jesus in this place. Bethlehem stories are restorative—they highlight faithful, God-loving people who got life right when so many others in Israel didn't. They are stories in which the Lord notices that his people are in trouble and responds by providing a solution. They are "feel-good" stories, and there is no Bethlehem story which makes us feel better than the account of Jesus's birth.

But this is not just a celebrative story about the birth of any baby boy; it is the story of the most important birth of all time. The son of Mary and Joseph is the Son of God sent to redeem the world. And there is only one place where this child could be born. The geography is critical because this Bethlehem story qualifies Jesus to be that descendant of David who would rule an eternal kingdom and rescue the world from sin. This is the best solution story of all.

The walk from Nazareth to Bethlehem is the first one we take with Jesus in this book. We have been to Bethlehem before—it is a place that fills us with positive feelings and one significant expectation. This is where Jesus, the solution for our sin, will be born.

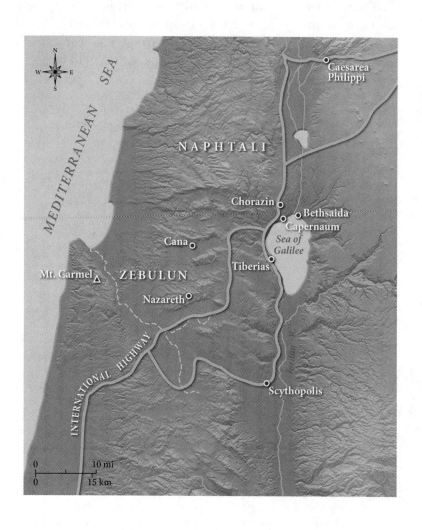

3

WALKING WITH JESUS AROUND NAZARETH

THE LONGER WE SPEND IN a place, the more it comes to define who we are. That was true of Jesus as well. When we start matching footsteps with him, we find ourselves walking around one place more than any other—the small village of Nazareth.

Jesus visited many places where he stayed for a few hours or days. But he lived in Nazareth for decades. Surprisingly, this created a real public relations problem for him.

People did not expect much from Nazareth. And those low expectations were projected onto everyone who lived there. Why would Jesus walk around this place for so long when it cost him the respect of others? Matthew seems to give us an answer when he says Jesus's stay in Nazareth fulfilled Old Testament prophecy. But this statement turns out to be just as perplexing as Jesus's decision to live in Nazareth. There is no Old Testament prophecy that directly connects the place name "Nazareth" with the Messiah.

So it sounds like we have some work to do if we are going to understand Jesus's long stay in Nazareth and the perplexing prophecy claim of Matthew. The best way to get to the bottom of both is to spend time walking around Nazareth with Jesus.

What was this town like in his day? On our maps we find Nazareth in the region of Lower Galilee, on the southernmost of a series of east-west ridges. What our maps show less clearly is that the village is not perched on the top of this ridge, overlooking the expansive Jezreel Valley to the south, but rather sits at the bottom of a small valley carved into the ridge. Nazareth sat in a geographical bowl that fostered the cultural isolation that characterized the village. Unless they had climbed the ridge, no one could see into

Nazareth from the outside—and people in Nazareth could not see out into the world.

Geography not only blocked the view, it also limited the growth of Nazareth. This isolated village of subsistence farmers reached a population ceiling predetermined by the amount of surrounding farmland. Nazareth did not import food products, so it could grow only as large as the local farmland would allow—and this capped the size of the village at about three or four hundred people.

When we walk around first-century Nazareth, it will not take long. The village occupies only about four acres on which a dozen or so homes have been built. It is true that the International Highway connecting the region with the markets of Asia, Africa, and Europe is only ten miles away; but it might as well be a thousand miles. Nazareth sits in a topographic bowl better suited to isolation than connection. The world seeks nothing from Nazareth, and Nazareth seeks nothing from the world.

This geographical and cultural isolation, cutting Nazareth off from the mainstream, explains the low expectations people had toward its native sons and daughters. Nothing of historical significance happened here. It is unmentioned in the Old Testament. It is unmentioned in Jewish traditional writings. It is even unmentioned by the first-century historian, Josephus, although he did describe a battle that occurred in the vicinity. Aside from Jesus, no one of historical significance came from this village.

The fact of the matter is that if we were not walking with Jesus, we would really have no reason to visit Nazareth. There is nothing interesting to see or do. No one expects much from the place or its people.

Three examples from the life of Jesus show how his longtime association with Nazareth caused low expectations to cling to him. First, when Philip told Nathanael that he had found the long-awaited Messiah and identified him as "Jesus of Nazareth" (John 1:45), Nathanael could hardly contain himself. He exclaimed, "Nazareth! Can anything good come from there?" (John 1:46).

Nathanael had grown up in Cana, a village of similar size one ridge north of Nazareth. Other Galileans like him questioned the idea of a Messiah from Nazareth, but so did Judeans. Their low expectations of Galileans in general and people from Nazareth in particular were coupled with the fact that they knew the Messiah was to come from one of their towns: Bethlehem. Jesus's extended stay in Nazareth led many to assume he had been born there, so Judeans often dismissed him out of hand (John 7:41–43).

Romans also knew the low expectations associated with Nazareth, and they referenced them at the time of Jesus's crucifixion. Judean religious leaders had prodded Pilate to act against Jesus; the Roman governor, tired of their manipulative actions and words, looked for a way to get back at them. So he fashioned a sign that was posted on Jesus's cross, combining the village name from which Jesus had come with the charge the Jewish leaders had leveled against him: "JESUS OF NAZARETH, THE KING OF THE JEWS" (John 19:19). This preposterous combination of geography and royalty was so offensive to the Jewish leaders that they insisted it be changed. Pilate, done being manipulated, simply said, "What I have written, I have written" (John 19:22).

Why did the heavenly Father put his Son in this position? Why create this public relations nightmare for Jesus by linking him so intimately with Nazareth? The gospel writer Matthew, who had walked with Jesus and seen the challenge Nazareth presented, offers a pair of sentences to explain the Father's actions: "He went and lived in a town called Nazareth. So was fulfilled what was said through the prophets, that he would be called a Nazarene" (2:23).

Matthew defends Jesus's longtime connection to Nazareth by saying it fulfilled an Old Testament promise about him. But this simple answer runs into all kinds of trouble when we look at it more closely. To be sure, Matthew has a habit of connecting Old Testament promises about the coming Messiah with things that Jesus says and does. But this particular statement creates a problem: there is no language precisely like this in the Old Testament or, for that matter, in any of the Jewish traditional writings. In fact, there is no mention of Nazareth at all in the Old Testament.

So how do we settle this question? Let's take a look at two proposed solutions.

Some scholars have said that Matthew has in mind the Old Testament law regarding the Nazirite vow (Numbers 6:1–21). During the time of this vow, the law directs the vow taker to be distinguished from others by avoiding products associated with the grapevine (like grapes and wine), contact with the deceased, and haircuts. In virtually all cases, the Nazirite experience was time-limited; one exception was Samson, who lived his entire life as a Nazirite (Judges 13:5). But it seems unlikely that this is what Matthew is thinking. What is missing is any statement that this Nazirite status would somehow apply to the Messiah. Furthermore, the Gospels do not indicate that Jesus lived the unique life of those who were under a Nazirite vow.

Another proposal suggests that Matthew is using a play on words, linking Jesus with Old Testament prophecies that describe the Messiah as the Branch. For example, Isaiah 11:1 announces, "A shoot will come up from the stump of Jesse; from his roots a Branch will bear fruit." The supposed play on words is the similarity in sound between the name of the village, Nazareth, and the Hebrew word for branch, *nêtser*. This is an interesting solution, but does not address the fact that the language of Matthew says Jesus's *physical presence* in Nazareth fulfills Old Testament expectations about him.

A third explanation takes geography into account and helps explain the long stay of Jesus in Nazareth. When we look carefully at Matthew's language, two things stand out. First, he is not discussing a single statement made by a particular prophet, but about a set of statements made "through the prophets"—note the plural. This is the only time that Matthew uses this formula for introducing Old Testament prophecy, and it means we ought to look for a thematic statement about the Messiah found in more than one Old Testament passage. Matthew indicates that the fulfilled prophecy is intimately connected to the fact that Jesus lived in Nazareth and was called a "Nazarene"—I think the church father Eusebius is correct when he wrote early in the fourth century that this label, Nazarene, simply identifies Jesus as someone who came from Nazareth.

Maybe you are thinking, *I have not been here before.* In one way that is true—as a reader of the Old Testament, you have not been to this village before since it is unmentioned in the text. But, on the other hand, the language of prophetic expectation has taken us to a village just like this.

The prophets have told us to look for a Messiah with all the markings of someone who comes from a village like Nazareth. We don't have the village's name, but we do have the template. The Messiah will live in a place that diminishes expectations about him. We are sent looking for someone who is more often despised than celebrated, an idea clearly stated in Isaiah's well-known words about the Messiah: "He grew up before him like a tender shoot, and like a root out of dry ground. He had no beauty or majesty to attract us to him, nothing in his appearance that we should desire him. He was despised and rejected by mankind, a man of suffering, and familiar with pain. Like one from whom people hide their faces he was despised, and we held him in low esteem" (Isaiah 53:2–3). This expectation is also communicated in other Old Testament passages linked to the coming Messiah, including Psalm 22:6–7 and 69:8, Isaiah 49:7, and Daniel 9:26.

As we walk with Jesus, we spend many years with him in Nazareth. We see that the low expectations associated with this farm village are transferred to him, and that means Jesus of Nazareth fits the expectation of the Old Testament prophets. The Messiah is someone who will call attention to himself by the very fact that he calls so little attention to himself. This is the defining characteristic of someone from Nazareth. So Jesus's association with Nazareth further confirms his claim to the title of Messiah, our Savior from sin.

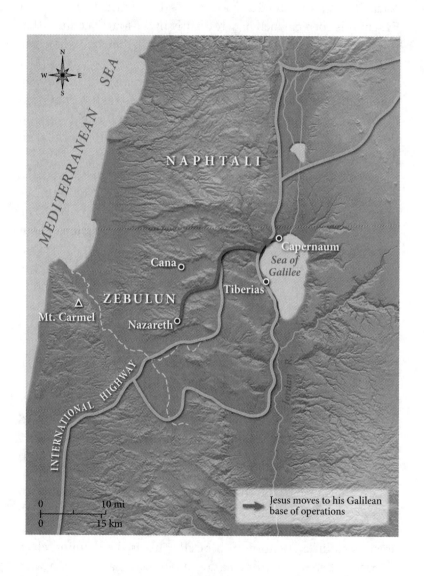

4

WALKING WITH JESUS FROM NAZARETH TO CAPERNAUM

AVERAGE AMERICANS MOVE MORE THAN eleven times in their lives. You may well be among those who have experienced a move prompted by changes in work, family, or economic status.

People in Bible times moved much less frequently. In fact, many people lived their entire lives—from birth through childhood, marriage, parenting, and death—in the same village. People in Jesus's day only moved when they had a very good reason for doing so.

That makes the move of Jesus from Nazareth to Capernaum both unusual and noteworthy. So Matthew gives it special attention and an explanation (4:12–17).

As we walk with Jesus from one town to the other, things start to look familiar—we have been here before. Although Capernaum is not mentioned by name in the Old Testament, this region appears in a prophecy about the Messiah written seven hundred years before Jesus's birth. He fulfilled this prophecy when he moved from Nazareth to Capernaum.

The relocation of Jesus is preceded by a flurry of moves in Matthew 3 and the early verses of chapter four. After leaving Nazareth, the first stop is the Jordan River near the ford opposite Jericho, where John the Baptist was preaching and teaching. Jesus walked here to ask John to baptize him, a sign that marked the start of Jesus's public ministry (3:13). Then, just as quickly, we are off to the nearby Judean Wilderness.

The Holy Spirit led Jesus into this forbidding landscape where he faced the first temptation of Satan (4:1). Two more temptations quickly followed in other locations, first at the temple in Jerusalem and then on a very high mountain, likely Mount Hermon on the far northern border of Israel (4:5, 8). After rushing from one end of the Promised Land to the other, we return to Nazareth.

Matthew lets us catch our breath here, but only for the time it takes to read one verse. Then we make one more move, which stands out because it is more permanent in nature. In Matthew's words, "Leaving Nazareth, [Jesus] went and lived in Capernaum" (4:13). Rapid movement has given way to relocation. Capernaum is described as "his own town" (Matthew 9:1) and as his new "home" (Mark 2:1).

Map labels like "Nazareth" and "Capernaum" do not reveal just how dramatically these two towns differed. Let's see how much by considering four points of contrast.

First, Nazareth and Capernaum differed topographically. As we've seen, Nazareth was geographically isolated, tucked into a valley at the top of a high ridge. Capernaum was out in the open, sprawling on a plain next to the Sea of Galilee and astride the International Highway.

Second, Nazareth and Capernaum differed in size. While the terrain restricted Nazareth to the status of a village with no more than four hundred residents, Capernaum could stretch out and become a town of more than fifteen hundred.

Third, the economies of these towns looked different. Nazareth had a self-contained economy: you ate what you grew and you wore clothing produced from local livestock. Capernaum was a town with a broader economic base and international connections. In addition to farming, its people were involved in fishing on the Sea of Galilee and the processing of those fish for sale outside the region. Capernaum's basalt was very durable, and a collection of local artisans became skilled in shaping this stone into tools, including grain grinding mills that sustained their shape in heavy use; these were marketed well outside of Capernaum. Additionally, the International Highway that connected the markets of Africa and Europe passed just outside of town, so some in Capernaum formed businesses that provided support for those traveling the highway. Capernaum had a very sophisticated economy compared to Nazareth.

Fourth, there was a difference in the nature of those who lived in the two towns. Observant Jewish families seeking isolation from the increasingly Romanized world of the Promised Land found their haven in Nazareth. This was a village in which you would see the same faces every day because strangers were rare. By contrast, Capernaum had a mixed population of Jews and Gentiles, and visitors were the norm rather than the exception.

Overall, Nazareth was an inward-looking place, unengaged with the larger world. Capernaum was just the opposite. When Jesus moved to Capernaum, he landed in the place that was very different from the one in which he had grown up.

So why would Jesus make such a relocation? There are two reasons. First, the move changed the level of access people had to what Jesus said and did. If he had remained in Nazareth, the geography and culture would have resisted the spread of news about him. Capernaum, sitting on an open plain, had a larger and more diverse population that entertained travelers from throughout the world—and in an era without electronic communication, the news of the day spread with such travelers, particularly merchants moving goods along the International Highway.

You can imagine that the things happening around Capernaum during the early first century were among the most tantalizing news items of the day. An ordinary looking Jewish man, claiming to be the Son of God on a mission to save the world from sin, was saying things quite unlike any other teacher had ever said. And he supported his claims with one miracle after another. This information had importance for people far from isolated Nazareth, so Jesus went to live in Capernaum to make sure the news about him spread widely—even to places like the ones where you and I have lived. Everyone who has come to know Jesus did, in part, because he left Nazareth and moved to Capernaum.

Here is the second purpose in Jesus's walk to Capernaum: Matthew notes that this change in residence fulfills an Old Testament prophecy, one with a geographical component. "Leaving Nazareth, he went and lived in Capernaum, which was on the lake shore *in the area of Zebulun. This is in addition to the area of Naphtali* in order to fulfill what was said through the prophet Isaiah: 'Land of Zebulun and land of Naphtali, the Way of the Sea, the land beyond the Jordan, Galilee of the Gentiles—the people living in darkness have seen a great light; for those living in the land of the shadow of death a light has dawned'" (Matthew 4:13–16, translation and emphasis mine). Note how the regions of Zebulun and Naphtali are mentioned twice, in that order. The geographical components of this prophecy are critical, so it is important we get them right.

Look carefully at your Bible's wording and compare it to the italics of my translation. Many English translations will have phrasing like "by the lake in the area of Zebulun and Naphtali." This way of translating makes Matthew's point more difficult to see, because it makes it sound as if Capernaum is in two geographical areas, Zebulun and Naphtali, at the same time. But that is not the case. Zebulun and Naphtali are labels for two different regions, parcels of land assigned to two of the twelve tribes of Israel (Joshua 19:10–16, 32–39). These regions are important to our discussion because they correspond to the locations of Nazareth and Capernaum. If we plot the location of Nazareth, we will find it located in the tribal territory of Zebulun; Capernaum is within the tribal territory of Naphtali. That means when Jesus moved from Nazareth to Capernaum, he was moving from Zebulun to Naphtali.

Why is this important? Because we have been here before. Isaiah declared that when the Messiah arrived in the Promised Land, he would have a sustained presence in these two tribal territories, changing the way people perceived them (9:1–2). In Isaiah's time, things were not going well in Zebulun and Naphtali; they had felt the humiliation, disruption, and pain associated with the invasion of the Assyrian empire and the policies it imposed on them (2 Kings 15:29; 17:24–41). There were so many non-Jews living in these tribal territories that the area became known as "Galilee of the Gentiles." It was perceived as a place commingled with darkness and death.

But Isaiah saw that a new era would dawn. When the Messiah arrived, he would change things for the better by bringing "light" to dark places. "Arise, shine, for your light has come, and the glory for the LORD rises upon you. See, darkness covers the earth and thick darkness is over the peoples, but the LORD rises upon you and his glory appears over you. Nations will come to your light, and kings to the brightness of your dawn" (Isaiah 60:1–3). Jesus identifies himself as that "light" (John 9:5).

But where would that light appear? Isaiah 9 tells us to expect that "light" to shine brightly in two tribal territories, Zebulun and Naphtali. Jesus spent the early years of his life in Nazareth, in the tribal territory of Zebulun. When he moved from Nazareth to Capernaum, he moved to Naphtali, fulfilling the second half of Isaiah's prophecy about the Messiah.

We take many walks with Jesus in the gospel of Matthew. This one is recounted so briefly we might well miss it: "Leaving Nazareth, he went and lived in Capernaum." But if we understand the geography, this is a thunderclap. We have been here before, when the prophet Isaiah brought us to Zebulun and Naphtali and said it is where the world's Light would dawn.

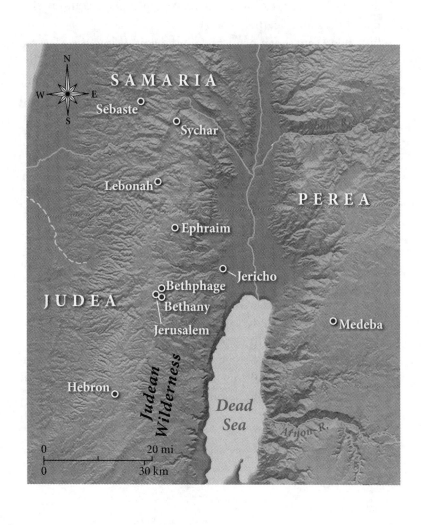

5

WALKING WITH JESUS FROM JERICHO TO BETHPHAGE

OUR NEXT WALK WITH JESUS is going to be physically challenging. It begins in Jericho, proceeds west through the Judean Wilderness, stops for the night at Bethany, and then continues the next morning to Bethphage, where we climb up and over the Mount of Olives to Jerusalem (Luke 19:1, 11, 29). It is a long walk, charged with emotion and filled with intensity.

Jesus says this walk will be his last. It will end in his rejection by the Jewish leadership, his suffering and death and resurrection (Luke 9:22). But, without a hint of hesitation, "Jesus resolutely set out for Jerusalem" (Luke 9:51).

It would be easy to get ahead of ourselves, running quickly to the dramatic events that unfold within Jerusalem. But let's not. Instead, let's focus on the segment of the journey that takes us from Jericho to Bethphage. Thinking about where we are, we will see that this walk fulfills three separate Old Testament prophecies about the Messiah.

We start this walk at the bottom of the Jordan River valley, near the location where Jesus was baptized three years earlier. We enter Jericho, the city in which Jesus helps people from different ends of the socioeconomic spectrum. First, he heals an impoverished blind man begging along the roadside (Luke 18:35–43). Shortly afterward, along the same road, Jesus calls out to Zacchaeus, a man small in stature but not in wealth, who had climbed a sycamore tree to get a better look. From that tree, we will walk to the home of this chief tax collector and watch as his life is completely changed in an evening (Luke 19:1–10).

The next day, Jesus starts early with a hike that leads from Jericho toward Jerusalem. This will be a full day of travel on one of Israel's most challenging roads. The fifteen-mile trail between Jericho and Jerusalem is rocky, uneven, and mercilessly hot. It takes us through the hostile realm of the Judean Wilderness where water is scarce just where we need it most. We repeatedly climb, descend, and climb again on our way to the Holy City—by the time we reach Jerusalem, we will have climbed more than 3,400 feet. But it feels even longer because of all those times we ascend a ridge only to give up the gain by descending into the next canyon.

Dirty, sweaty, and tired, we feel a rush of relief as Bethany comes into view. This is not our ultimate goal, but we are not going to Jerusalem today. It would be very difficult to find a place to stay there, you see—we are making this walk with Jesus at the time of the Passover festival, and Jerusalem is filled with Jewish pilgrims. This raises the rates and lowers the availability of lodging in the city. So Jesus decides to stay in Bethany on the southeast flanks of the Mount of Olives.

This puts him less than an hour's walk from Jerusalem—and gives Jesus the chance to stay in the home of his dear friends, Mary, Martha, and Lazarus. It is Saturday evening, time to rest up because tomorrow is a big day (John 12).

The walk from Bethany to Jerusalem is a little less than two miles, but it requires us to climb over the two-mile-long ridge of the Mount of Olives, which rises nearly 2,700 feet. The climb is strenuous but nothing like the walk of the previous day. As we near the top of the ridge, Jesus does something we have not seen him do before. He sends two of his disciples ahead to secure a donkey for him to ride into the little village of Bethphage, the end of this leg of the journey (Luke 19:28–36).

It does not seem like much of a destination. Today, the meager archaeological remains suggest that there was not much here in the first century when Jesus arrived. Bethphage is a rather unre-markable village with an unfamiliar name—if you are wondering why you don't recognize it, the town is mentioned only three times in the entire Bible. Each reference relates to this story of Jesus's final entry into Jerusalem (Matthew 21:1; Mark 11:1; Luke 19:29).

To understand why we have walked here with Jesus, there is one crucial fact we need to know about this village: Bethphage marks the eastern city limits of Jerusalem. At first, this may not seem to make sense. We often think of Jerusalem's city limits as marked by the defensive walls built close to the bustling urban center, or perhaps by an easily distinguished topographical feature like the Kidron Valley. Yet throughout Jerusalem's history, residents considered the western slope of the Mount of Olives—even though it lay outside the walls and on the far side of the valley—as connected to their city. The northern part of this ridge was particularly fit for growing olives; the southern slope, chalky and unfit for agriculture, was the perfect place to dig graves. From the time of David to the time of Jesus, this was Jerusalem's cemetery. And it makes sense that people would think of the western slope of the Mount of Olives as "Jerusalem," because this is where their deceased family members were.

The places we encounter on this long walk from Jericho to Bethphage are places that we, as readers of the Old Testament, have been before. It is time to reconsider this walk through the lens of the geographic prophecies made about the Messiah.

Think about the road between Jericho and Jerusalem. This road lies east of Jerusalem, in the Judean Wilderness, and here is why that is important: Old Testament believers expected the Messiah to arrive in Jerusalem from the east. Malachi urged his listeners to look east for the "sun of righteousness will rise with healing in its rays" (4:2). Isaiah added even more precision to this expectation—from the perspective of Jerusalem, the Messiah would arrive in Jerusalem from the east, by way of the Judean Wilderness. "Comfort, comfort my people, says your God," Isaiah wrote. "Speak tenderly to Jerusalem and proclaim to her that her hard service has been completed, that her sin has been paid for, that she has received from the LORD's hand double for all her sins. A voice of one calling: 'In the wilderness prepare the way for the LORD; make straight in the desert a highway for our God'" (40:1–3).

That means our walk from Jericho to Bethany to Bethphage has been more than just a way of getting to Jerusalem. The fact is, multiple road systems would have brought Jesus to Jerusalem. But on this last trip to the city, to certify his identity as the Messiah, Jesus intentionally approached Jerusalem from the east through the Judean Wilderness. We have been here before in the language of the prophets. This is the route we expect to see the Messiah walking.

A second prophecy fulfilled in this walk states that the Messiah will make an official, attention-grabbing *entry* into Jerusalem. Again, we find this prophecy in Isaiah, who speaks about the rehabilitation of the Holy City, Zion, following its horrific destruction during the invasion of the Babylonian empire. The most striking thing about the rebuilt city would be the official arrival of Messiah himself. It was going to be very public and impossible to miss: "Say to Daughter Zion, 'See, your Savior comes! See, his reward is with him, and his recompense accompanies him'" (Isaiah 62:11).

Jesus had been to Jerusalem many times in his life. In obedience to the Torah, he would have traveled to Jerusalem at least three times a year for the high Jewish festivals (Deuteronomy 16:16), though the great majority of those trips are not reported in the Bible. The accounts we do have never distinguish Jesus from other people entering the Holy City—until this time. As we walk with Matthew and Jesus into Bethphage, the gospel writer turns to us and says, "This took place to fulfill what was spoken through the prophet: 'Say to Daughter Zion, "See, your king comes to you"'" (21:4–5). Jesus had just made the long-awaited, official entry into Jerusalem as promised by Isaiah.

There is one more Old Testament prophecy to mention. Zechariah says that this dramatic entry of the Messiah into Jerusalem will find him riding a donkey: "Rejoice greatly, Daughter Zion!

Shout, Daughter Jerusalem! See, your king comes to you, righteous and victorious, lowly and riding on a donkey, on a colt, the foal of a donkey" (9:9). Now notice the careful language Luke uses to describe what Jesus did. He sent two disciples ahead to secure a donkey from Bethphage, for the only time we read about Jesus riding any pack animal. Luke stresses the importance of this detail by repeating the phrase, "the Lord needs it" twice in this brief account (Luke 19:31, 34).

Realize how strange this must have looked. Jesus has just spent perhaps twenty to twenty-five minutes walking uphill, toward the top of the Mount of Olives. He is about to crest the ridge and begin the walk down into the urban sprawl of Jerusalem. If there was a time to get a donkey, it was when he *started* the journey at the bottom of the ridge—not once he'd reached the top!

The "need" was not about saving energy but about entering Jerusalem. And this is where our understanding of the Old Testament and Bethphage come together. To fulfill the prophecy of Zechariah, Jesus had to ride a donkey across the line of Jerusalem's city limits, from the east side. Notice that Luke strives for extreme geographic clarity here, saying that Jesus sent the disciples *ahead* to Bethphage and they *brought the donkey back* to Jesus before he entered the town (19:29–30, 35). When he rode the donkey into the village of Bethphage—the eastern edge of Jerusalem—the hillside exploded with a dramatic welcome.

When we walk along this road with Jesus, we understand why the people were so excited that day. The geography tells the story— Jesus is making good on three promises made about the Messiah. He is making his official entry into Jerusalem, from the east and through the wilderness, by riding a donkey into Bethphage. The prophets had taken us here before, telling us to expect nothing less.

God put prophecies about the coming Messiah in our Bibles to help us identify the one individual who can save us from our sins. He knew we would need more information than was offered in the language of the first promise of the Messiah, in Genesis 3:15.

This verse asserts that the Lord would send an individual to rescue the world from sin, but says only that this person would be a descendant of Eve. The language is so broad that any human being would qualify. So the Lord began to narrow those who qualified through a series of Old Testament prophecies: the true Messiah would have a certain family history, demonstrate his authority with miracles, and fulfill certain geographic realities like the ones we have just studied.

Jesus did not drop into the world unexpectedly. His arrival and life conformed to a very detailed grid of Old Testament prophecies, and he challenged people to look for those connections: "You study the Scriptures diligently because you think that in them you have eternal life. These are the very Scriptures that testify about me" (John 5:39). Among the last things Jesus said to the disciples before his ascension into heaven was this: "This is what I told you while I was still with you: Everything must be fulfilled that is written about me in the Law of Moses, the Prophets and the Psalms" (Luke 24:44).

So there is value for us in walking along the road with Jesus, looking for places linked to Old Testament prophecy. The pretenders have not gone away. There are many religious people who claim to offer the path to successful living and salvation. You would not be the first Christian to ask questions like these: Have I lined up with the right religion? Is Jesus all that he claimed to be? Am I really forgiven, or have I been taken in by a fraud? But the Old Testament prophecies about the Messiah help answer those questions.

During the thousands of years that anticipated Jesus's coming,

God the Father created a matrix of prophecies about him, many of which have a geographical component. When we see Jesus doing exactly what God promised the Messiah would do *in those places*, we know we have put our faith in the right Savior.

1. What can you do to make finding Old Testament geographical prophecies of the Messiah more apparent during your Bible reading and study time?

2. What is the most memorable insight you have obtained from studying the Bible stories in this section?

3. How has this part of the book changed the way you think about geography?

4. How has this part of the book changed the way you think about Jesus?

5. How can you use what you have learned here when introducing others to Jesus?

PART TWO

Jesus, Geography, and Substitution

I PLAYED BASKETBALL IN COLLEGE. And by my senior year, I started most games. That experience gave me a real appreciation for what it means to be on a team with well-prepared substitutes.

As a starter, my responsibility was to expend all the energy I could to get the team off to a good start. But before long, tired legs impaired my performance on offense and diminished my effectiveness on defense. That is when I needed a substitute, someone to replace me and do the things I could no longer do. My athletic experience helps me understand and appreciate the way the Bible introduces Jesus as my Substitute.

We all desperately need a substitute, in a contest much more serious than a basketball game. Human beings were the starters in this contest, which began in the Garden of Eden. But Adam and Eve did not last long—when challenged with temptation, they fell into sin. Ever since, the rest of us human beings have lived the legacy of their spiritual exhaustion. Their sin affected the entire human race, making us all liable to a punishment we do not want to endure. We owe the heavenly Father a level of loyalty and obedience that we cannot deliver. All of us need a substitute.

The good news is that we *have* a divine Substitute, who is ready to enter the contest in our place. Jesus lived that life of loyalty and obedience we owed but could not attain. Then he offered his loyalty and obedience to the Father as our substitute. As the apostle Paul described it in his letter to the church at Rome:

For just as through the disobedience of the one man
[Adam] the many were made sinners, so also through the
obedience of the one man [Jesus] the many will be made
righteous.

ROMANS 5:19

Jesus also suffered the punishment that should have been ours:

Surely he took up our pain and bore our suffering, yet we
considered him punished by God, stricken by him, and
afflicted. But he was pierced for our transgressions, he was
crushed for our iniquities; the punishment that brought us
peace was on him, and by his wounds we are healed. We
all, like sheep, have gone astray, each of us has turned to
our own way; and the LORD has laid on him the iniquity
of us all.

ISAIAH 53:4–6

Forgiveness belongs to us because Jesus came to earth as our
Substitute.

This news—of salvation by substitution—is so important that
the Bible speaks about it more than once and in more than one way.
Sometimes it is told in declarative sentences like those above. But
the Bible also teaches this substitution by using geography. That
is what this part of the book will explain.

As we walk along the road with Jesus, we find ourselves in
places we have walked before with the Children of Israel. These
points of geographic correspondence between Israel and Jesus are
important for two reasons. First, they demonstrate Jesus's ability
to serve as a substitute for mortals. He could not merely simulate
the human experience; he had to live it, and the geographic parallels we will study demonstrate that Jesus did just that. Second, we
learn from these stories that Jesus was not just willing and able to

be our substitute, but that he could succeed in exactly those circumstances and places where we fail. We need precisely that kind of Substitute—and these geographically oriented stories assure us that we have him.

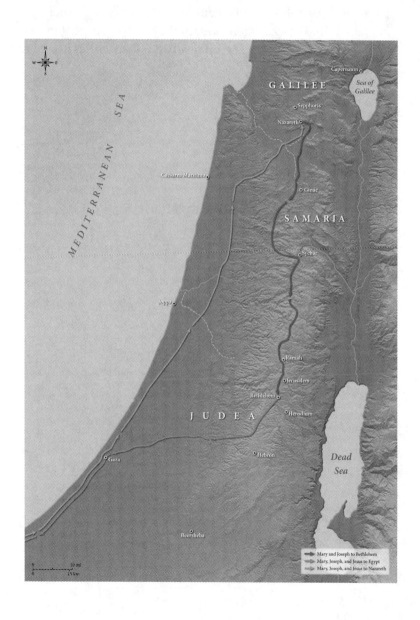

6

WALKING WITH JESUS
OUT OF EGYPT

LET'S WALK WITH JESUS TO and from Egypt, and along the way we'll find an example of substitution.

This is not one of the better-known stories from his life. But it is a story that makes a geographic connection with God's people of the past. Matthew highlights this parallel when he compares the experience of Jesus to that of Israel: "And so was fulfilled what the Lord had said through the prophet: 'Out of Egypt, I called my son'" (2:15).

This walk with Mary, Joseph, and Jesus is anything but a vacation. They are running from the Promised Land, fearing for their lives because of the mental instability and shocking cruelty of Herod the Great.

The Roman senate had appointed Herod king of Judea. He loved the honor and privilege that came with the title, but late in his life became paranoid of losing these benefits. When he sensed a threat to his throne, Herod was quick to murder the one he perceived to be a rival—even if it was a member of his own family.

That explains Herod's response to the news the Magi brought. They were looking for the newborn king of the Jews! Herod quietly put a plan into operation: he urged the Magi to find this child so that he too could "worship" him. Not so much—Herod wanted to find the child to execute him. When the Magi left, without having helped Herod with the identification, he quickly targeted all the boys up to two years old in greater Bethlehem (Matthew 2:16).

But before Herod could initiate this terrible plan, the angel of the Lord appeared to Joseph in a dream. "'Get up,' he said, 'take the child and his mother an escape to Egypt'" (Matthew 2:13).

Egypt had a couple of advantages to offer the holy family. First, there were other Jewish families among whom they might live. Centuries earlier, many Jews had fled the Promised Land for Egypt when the army of the Babylonian empire advanced against them (Jeremiah 43:4–7). Many stayed in Egypt, established homes, and started a new life. Places like Alexandria had a Jewish quarter that numbered in the tens of thousands at the time of Jesus. It is possible Mary, Joseph, and Jesus found refuge there. But that is just one of many Jewish centers in Egypt which could have provided them with a temporary home, among people cut from the same family stock.

The second advantage of Egypt was that it lay outside the reach and influence of Herod the Great. Earlier in his career, Herod had become a rival of Egypt's Cleopatra VII. Neither was inclined to do the other any favors. Although Cleopatra died in 30 BC, her animosity for Herod lived on in the Egyptian leaders who followed her. And that meant that Mary, Joseph, and Jesus were safely out of Herod's reach while in Egypt.

Of course, Egypt was not the Promised Land, so it would not be their permanent home. When Herod died, the angel of the Lord again appeared to Joseph, telling him that Herod was no longer a threat and that it was time for another long walk. "So he got up, took the child and his mother and went to the land of Israel" (Matthew 2:21).

Jesus, Mary, and Joseph left the Promised Land and walked to Egypt. Later, they returned to the Promised Land from Egypt. As we walk this pair of journeys with them, we get the feeling we have done this before. As readers of the Old Testament, we have.

The descendants of Abraham walked to Egypt in the time of his grandson Jacob. Jacob and his family left the Promised Land because a severe multiyear famine had gripped their home. Wells were not recharging, springs had gone dry, the fields produced no grain, and the trees produced no fruit. Something had to be done, and that something was a move to Egypt.

Egypt was also suffering from the famine, but two things made it a desirable place. First, its agriculture was dependent on the Nile River rather than direct rainfall. This river-based water supply created a much more durable ecosystem than the rain-based water system of Canaan. Consequently, it would recover more quickly from a time of famine than Canaan. The second thing making Egypt desirable was the fact that Jacob's beloved son, Joseph, was there. Though he had traveled there unwillingly, Joseph had risen to become second-in-command of all Egypt due to the Lord's blessing. God had informed Joseph of the coming famine, so he was able to store extra food during the good years preceding the trouble. Egypt had two things that Jacob desperately needed—food to eat and reunion with his son Joseph.

Despite all that Egypt offered, Jacob hesitated to go. His love for Joseph and the provision of Egypt drew him south. But he lingered at the border of Canaan because Egypt was not the land intimately linked to his family's divinely assigned mission (Genesis 12:1–3, 6–7). Only when the Lord spoke to Jacob in a nighttime vision did that change: "Do not be afraid to go down to Egypt, for I will make you into a great nation there. I will go down to Egypt with you, and I will surely bring you back again. And Joseph's own hand will close your eyes" (Genesis 46:3–4).

With this assurance, Jacob walked out of the Promised Land and took his entire family to Egypt. Here the Lord used the rich ecosystem of Egypt to provide food and protection for Jacob's people—not just for the few years of famine but for centuries to come. Egypt was not the Promised Land but, as promised, the Lord used it to grow this family of less than a hundred people into a nation that was counted in the tens of thousands.

Over time, their numbers gave the Egyptians pause, and the

country that fostered the Israelites' growth turned against them. Centuries after Jacob walked into Egypt, a new dynasty arose, one that saw Israel's large numbers as a threat to its national security. In a bid to limit their growth, Egypt subjected Israel to forced labor (Exodus 1:8–14). When that did not work, the king of Egypt directed the Hebrew midwives, and then "all his people," to kill every newborn boy (Exodus 1:15–22). It was time for Israel to return to the Promised Land. And that is exactly what the Lord told Moses (Exodus 6:6–8).

What follows is one of the most iconic moments in history. The Lord used ten devastating plagues to disrupt Egypt's economy, government stability, and confidence in its deities (Exodus 7–11). This led to the Israelites' walk out of Egypt, known simply as "the Exodus." Centuries after Jacob and his family walked the dusty trail from Canaan to Egypt, Moses reversed the journey. The Exodus is commemorated in many ways, including these words of Hosea: "When Israel was a child, I loved him, and out of Egypt I called my son" (11:1).

That language, quoted by Matthew, helps build the bridge between Jesus and Israel, both of whom made this trek to and from Egypt. When we dig deeper, the parallels are striking.

Both God's people of Old Testament times and Jesus faced a life-threatening circumstance in the Promised Land. God gave direct instructions—both to Jacob and to Jesus's human father, Joseph—to take their family from the Promised Land to Egypt. Both times the Lord used Egypt to provide a haven for those who left the Promised Land. When it was time, the Lord would again speak directly to Moses and Joseph, telling them to leave Egypt and return to the Promised Land.

As we walk to and from Egypt with the holy family, we get the feeling we have been here before. We have. And this sense of déjà vu is intended. Jesus travels the route from Israel to Egypt and back in order to identify with every human experience Israel had, even with the specific places they went. In this way, he demonstrates that he is both willing and able to serve as a substitute for mortals.

And, along the way, the words of Hosea achieve a more striking fulfillment: "When Israel was a child, I loved him, and out of Egypt I called my son" (11:1).

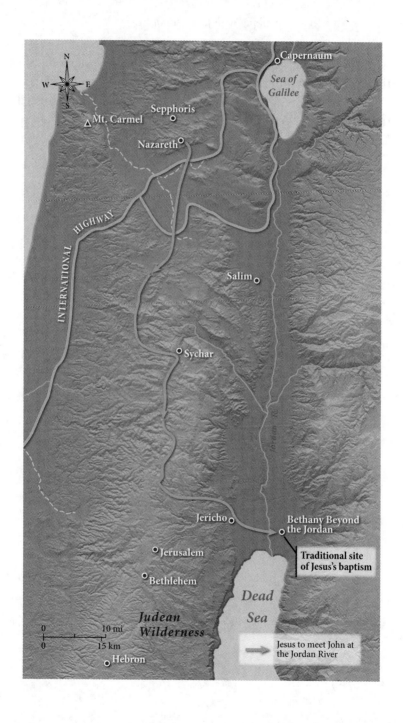

N
W E
S

Capernaum

Sea of
Galilee

Sepphoris

△ Mt. Carmel

Nazareth

INTERNATIONAL HIGHWAY

Salim

Sychar

Jericho

Bethany Beyond
the Jordan

Traditional site
of Jesus's baptism

Jerusalem

Bethlehem

Dead
Sea

Judean
Wilderness

0   10 mi
0   15 km

Hebron

Jesus to meet John at
the Jordan River

7

WALKING WITH JESUS
TO THE JORDAN RIVER

THE YOUNG MAN FROM NAZARETH is now an adult. It is harder to keep up with Jesus now—his strides are long and intentional as he leaves Galilee, headed for a ford of the Jordan River just north of the Dead Sea. We are on our way to meet Jesus's relative, John, who is preaching and baptizing there. Jesus is going to seek baptism from John.

When we arrive at the river, the place feels familiar. As Old Testament readers, we have been here before. This is the very spot where Joshua and the Israelites cross the Jordan, marking their entry—and the nation's reentry—into the Promised Land. When Jesus arrives here, we note another instance of geographic correspondence between him and the life of Israel. God the Father, as he had with Israel, uses the water of the Jordan River to confirm Jesus's unique identity and mark a transition point in his earthly mission.

John the Baptist plays a key role in this story. He was a relative of Jesus, but not just any relative—John was the special messenger the Old Testament prophets said we should expect, the one tasked with preparing people to meet the coming Savior. Isaiah characterized him as "a voice of one calling: 'In the wilderness prepare the way for the LORD; make straight in the desert a highway for our God'" (Isaiah 40:3). This messenger would be a person unlike any other, and Jesus confirmed that John the Baptist was that man (Luke 7:26–28).

In addition to speaking about the arrival of the Messiah, John was performing a special ritual called baptism. This baptism was distinct from any other water ritual of the Old Testament, and it was different than the baptism that Jesus directed his disciples to employ as he brought his ministry on earth to a close (Matthew 28:19–20). When people sought baptism from John, they were signifying their agreement with his teachings in general and their need to repent of their sins in particular. That is why it was called a "baptism of repentance" (Mark 1:4; Luke 3:3; Acts 13:24, 19:4). And that is why John objected when Jesus walked down to the river and asked his relative to baptize him.

The request seemed to get things backwards. Jesus did not need to repent, John did. Jesus did not need John's baptism, John needed Jesus's baptism (Matthew 3:14). But Jesus was persistent, and John yielded. "As soon as Jesus was baptized, he went up out of the water. At that moment heaven was opened, and he saw the Spirit of God descending like a dove and alighting on him. And a voice from heaven said, 'This is my Son, whom I love; with him I am well pleased'" (Matthew 3:16–17).

For the first time since the angels had lifted soaring songs above the Bethlehem fields, we see a heavenly announcement setting Jesus apart from every other human being. The Jesus who grew up in Nazareth looked very much like its other residents, and even as he approaches the Jordan for baptism, he looks like the hundreds of others who have come to John. But the time for anonymity is over. No one else's baptism ever ended in the way Jesus's baptism does. The heavenly Father uses this moment in Jesus's life to single him out from the crowd. He is identified in no uncertain terms as the promised Savior who would redeem all people from their sins.

With all that's going on around us, it's easy to lose track of where we are. So let's make sure we give this location a moment of our attention. Remember that Jesus has come to John while he is conducting his ministry in a region broadly defined as the Judean Wilderness (Matthew 3:1). The gospel of John is more precise, telling us that John was baptizing "at Bethany on the other side of the Jordan" (1:28). This is not the Bethany near Jerusalem, the home of Mary, Martha, and Lazarus.

In AD 333, a Christian traveler wrote that he had visited the site of Jesus's baptism, placing its location four and a half miles north of the Dead Sea. This is precisely where we find a number of Byzantine-era churches, near the location at which the earliest Christian map places this "Bethany on the other side of the Jordan."

The location makes sense. The Jordan becomes shallower here because tributaries from the east and west carry silt into the main channel of the river. The silt shallows the river, allowing travelers to walk across the natural ford that forms here. Most people in Jesus's day did not know how to swim, and they did not like the idea of crossing rivers that might require swimming. This was a big deal for average travelers, so much so that they would go literally miles out of their way to cross at a ford. And that is exactly what we have near Bethany beyond the Jordan—a natural ford in the Jordan, lying just east of Jericho.

River crossing! Jericho! Now we are really getting a sense of déjà vu in this location. We have been here before (Joshua 3–4). We have walked to this very spot with Joshua and the Israelites about fourteen hundred years earlier. At that time, Israel had formed a huge camp on the sprawling plain just east of the Jordan River, opposite Jericho. They did not intend to stay in the plain, but were preparing to cross the river and enter the Promised Land. It was a huge moment in Old Testament history because Abraham's descendants had spent four hundred years in Egypt and another forty years in the wilderness. Now, for the first time in centuries, the people were ready to reenter the land that was so intimately linked to their mission as a nation—to help repair the broken relationship between the world and the heavenly Father.

But things were not going well. The eyes of the Israelites moved back and forth between Joshua and the river. Neither left them feeling confident.

Moses—Israel's spiritual leader, a man who spoke directly with God—had just died. He was the man associated with miracle after miracle in the last decades. But now the younger, untested Joshua had replaced him. People undoubtedly had the same questions you and I might ask: Was the Lord really with Joshua as he had been with Moses? Could this man be all that Moses had been for the people?

Things did not look much better when their eyes turned from Joshua to the river. They were at a ford, but this was springtime when the river ran at flood stage. At other times of the year, the quiet flow at this ford posed no threat—people could make the crossing without getting water above their waist. Now, though, the river was running at ten feet in depth, upwards of a mile in width, and with a rushing current that no one wanted to measure. No one wanted to be first into the water for this crossing.

That is when the Lord stepped in, delivering a plan to Joshua that amazes to this day. At God's direction, the priests picked up the Ark of the Covenant and carried it to the water's edge. When their feet touched the surging water, the river was cut off far upstream and just stopped flowing. The priests then moved to the middle of the now-dry riverbed, perhaps glancing nervously northward, the direction from which the water had been cascading just moments earlier. The channel remained dry, so one by one— cautiously at first and then with growing confidence—all the other Israelites crossed the river on dry ground. After they were safely across, the priests left their spot in the middle of the riverbed. As soon as their feet touched the western bank, the frothing water roared back down the channel, tumbling and threatening as it had before. But that no longer mattered. Israel was safely across the Jordan. They were in the Promised Land.

This is where Jesus was baptized. Certainly, he had come here because he wanted to be baptized by John, and this was where John was doing his work. But there is more to the story than that: when we walk into this setting and feel the geographical déjà vu, we sense the symmetry between these events in the lives of Jesus and Joshua. Both involved the Jordan's flow—the water that had miraculously stopped at the time of Joshua was the same water John used to baptize Jesus. And both stories involved miracles that set a certain person or people apart from others.

Israel's miraculous crossing of the Jordan showed that this was no ordinary people group. That is made clear by the reaction of those on the west side of the river. "Now when all the Amorite kings west of the Jordan and all the Canaanite kings along the coast heard how the LORD had dried up the Jordan before the Israelites until they had crossed over, their hearts melted in fear and they no longer had the courage to face the Israelites" (Joshua 5:1). In the same way, the miraculous appearance of the Holy Spirit in the form of a dove and the booming voice of the heavenly Father marked Jesus as unique among people: "This is my Son, whom I love," God said, "with him I am well pleased" (Matthew 3:17).

In both stories, this place marked a transition. The Lord had repeatedly told the Israelites that crossing the Jordan River would initiate a new stage in their mission—it was the moment of Israel's reentry into the Promised Land. As the crossing grew closer, Moses stated this notion repeatedly—the Lord was leading them to the Jordan so they could cross into the land promised to Abraham, Isaac, and Jacob (Deuteronomy 4:14, 21–22, 26; 6:1, 9:1; 11:8, 31; 12:10; 27:2–3; 30:17–18; 31:3, 13; 32:47). In the same way, Jesus's baptism marks a transition in his life. Gone are the quiet days in Nazareth, the times when people saw him as little more than the kid from the neighborhood. His baptism marked Jesus unmistakably as the Savior from sin. His public ministry was now underway.

When we walk to the Jordan River for Jesus's baptism, we get the sense we have been here before. That is intentional. Jesus comes to this ford in the Jordan opposite Jericho because Israel had been here earlier. Jesus intentionally replicates the experiences of Israel, in specific locations, to demonstrate his role as the Substitute.

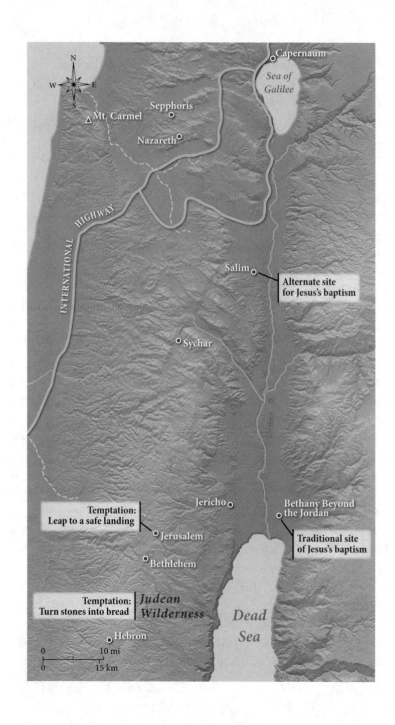

8

WALKING WITH JESUS
INTO THE WILDERNESS

WE WILL TAKE TWO MORE walks with Jesus in this part of the book. Both move us closer to understanding how Jesus saves by being our Substitute.

These walks, like the first two, lead to places we have been before with Israel. But here we find even more than geographic correspondence between that nation and the life of Jesus. These next two walks lead to places where Israel's faith failed the Father's test.

Jesus places himself in the same geographic circumstances, confronts the same tests, and succeeds where Israel failed. The gospel writers report this success not to make the failings of Israel even more apparent, but to highlight Jesus's role as the Substitute for sinners. As the writer of Hebrews said, "We do not have a high priest who is unable to empathize with our weaknesses, but we have one who has been tempted in every way, just as we are—yet he did not sin" (4:15).

Our first stop is the harshest, driest, most rugged and threatening landscape we will walk with Jesus. Matthew gives us little time to enjoy and reflect on the stunning moment of Jesus's baptism before he whisks us off into the nearby Judean Wilderness. The terrain is positively treacherous, with steep mountainsides plunging into narrow canyons. One misstep could easily result in a fatal fall.

The scarce rain here tumbles as quickly as a careless hiker down to the bottom of the canyon. Limited water and nutrient-poor soil join to make this a landscape with few plants—those that hold on don't provide enough nutrition to sustain human settlement but they do meet the needs of a few desert-dwelling animals like the ibex. Of course, where there are prey animals, there will be predators. The wilderness area we are walking with Jesus is home to mountain lions and wolves that eye hikers as just another meal in this austere region. Walk to one of the high ridges and strain your eyes in any direction—you will find the same geographic reality no matter where you look. This is a land of little water, no grain, and multiple threats to mortal existence.

It is no accident that Jesus walked into this hostile ecosystem; he came here to be tempted by the devil (Matthew 4:1–4). For the first time since the Lord had promised Eve that one of her descendants would do battle with Satan (Genesis 3:15), the devil got a clear look at his opponent. In the centuries preceding, Satan had defeated every single descendant of Eve—even the great ones, like Moses and David, had sinned. The devil mistakenly perceived Jesus would be as vulnerable to temptation as they were—especially since he had weakened himself physically and mentally by a fast of forty days.

Satan's calculated approach is strikingly similar to the one he used in the Garden of Eden: it involved food. Jesus's body was demanding nutrition in a land that naturally offered none. The devil urged Jesus to solve the problem himself rather than trust his Father. "If you are the Son of God," Satan said, "tell these stones to become bread" (Matthew 4:3).

When we note this wilderness context for Jesus's temptation, we feel déjà vu—we have been here before with Israel. Matthew wants to be sure that we connect these two temptation stories. So he emphasizes five points of similarity between the experiences of Israel and Jesus.

The first involves how they got to the wilderness. The Lord led Israel out of Egypt and into the wilderness (Deuteronomy 8:2), using a pillar of cloud by day and a pillar of fire by night (Exodus 13:22). Jesus's entry into the wilderness is described in the same way: he was led by the Spirit (Matthew 4:1).

The second parallel has to do with place. The Lord led Israel into wilderness areas which have a variety of names, such as Shur, Sin, Sinai, Paran, and Zin (Exodus 15:22; 16:1; 19:1; Numbers 12:16; 20:1). This is not the same wilderness region in which Jesus was tempted; these places are far to the south of where Jesus conducted his ministry. In this case, the geographical parallel is not found in the specific place but in the type of ecosystem. Jesus would experience all the same threats that Israel faced centuries earlier.

The third parallel is found in the length of time, in periods of forty. The wilderness is hostile to human existence, so smart travelers always minimize risk by limiting the amount of time spent there. In an ironic turn, that is not the case with either Israel or Jesus. Israel spent forty years in its wilderness (Deuteronomy 2:7). Jesus spent forty days and forty nights there (Matthew 4:2).

The fourth parallel naturally follows from the place and length of time. Both Israel and Jesus were humbled as they reached the horizon of human limitations imposed by wilderness. Israel was humbled by hunger (Deuteronomy 8:3, 16). Jesus allowed himself to experience this same wilderness-imposed hunger. Matthew's simple words, "he was hungry" (4:2), underrepresent the experience of Jesus. Hunger pangs ravaged his body and distracted his thinking, and it was here—nearly six weeks into his fast—that the temptation came.

The fifth parallel is this: the heavenly Father basically asks both Israel and Jesus, "Will you trust me even when the fundamentals for survival are not in view?" That question is not a direct quotation from Scripture, but it lives in both of these stories. The Lord had brought the Israelites into the wilderness to humble them, to test them, and to teach them. That is how Moses described their extended stay: "Remember how the LORD your God led you all the way in the wilderness these forty years, *to humble* and *test* you in order to know what was in your heart, whether or not you would keep his commands. He *humbled* you, causing you to hunger and then feeding you with manna, which neither you nor your ancestors had known, *to teach* you that man does not live on bread alone but on every word that comes from the mouth of the LORD" (Deuteronomy 8:2–3, emphasis added). *Will you trust me when the fundamentals for survival are not in view?* The question hangs over Jesus's temptation in the wilderness as well. "Are you really going to stay hungry and wait for your Father to provide when you, the Son of God, are fully capable of turning all these stones into nice, warm loaves of bread?" Jesus had put himself in the same situation that Israel had been in, centuries earlier.

At this point of the story, Israel and Jesus part company. Israel failed to answer the question well, no matter which wilderness area they were in.

In the Desert of Sin, the people complained about Moses's leadership and the Lord's plan: "If only we had died by the LORD's hand in Egypt! There we sat around pots of meat and ate all the food we wanted, but you have brought us out into this desert to starve this entire assembly to death" (Exodus 16:3). Even years later, the wilderness experience had not produced a sustained trust in the Father's provision. Now in the Desert of Zin, their desire to leave the wilderness unchanged is clearly communicated in these words: "If only we had died when our brothers fell dead before the LORD! Why did you bring the LORD's community into this wilderness, that we and our livestock should die here? Why did you bring us up out of Egypt to this terrible place? It has no grain or figs, grapevines or pomegranates. And there is no water to drink!" (Numbers 20:3–5). The Lord had brought Israel into the wilderness to humble and test the people. Their responses show just how badly they failed the test. God asked, "Will you trust me even when the fundamentals for survival are not in view?" Israel's answer was an unmistakable, "No!"

As we walk with Jesus into the wilderness, seeing that he has put himself into exactly the same geographical, physical, and emotional circumstances as Israel, we wonder: will he get this right?

Satan quickly challenges Jesus, urging him to act on his own rather than trust the Father: "If you are the Son of God, tell these stones to become bread" (Matthew 4:3). Now, there is no moral issue in using a miracle to generate food. In fact, Jesus performed food miracles on two other occasions later in his ministry, multiplying bread to feed thousands. But this is different—it is not just about food, but about trusting the heavenly Father to provide, even in the harshest of ecosystems.

There in the wilderness, we watch Jesus as he stares straight into the tempter's eyes. Without missing a beat, Jesus delivers his answer, quoting the very words Moses had used centuries earlier to explain the purpose of a wilderness experience: "It is written: 'Man shall not live on bread alone, but on every word that comes from the mouth of God'" (Matthew 4:4). This is a place to learn and demonstrate trust.

So why would Jesus go to the trouble and hardship of replicating this experience of Israel in the wilderness? Certainly, his actions show us how to defeat the devil's temptations by using the Word of God. But I need more than an example to follow—I need someone to do for me what I cannot do on my own.

And that is what Jesus's time in the wilderness teaches. He went out to be tested because the Lord had led Israel into the wilderness to test them. And in precisely the circumstances in which Israel had repeatedly failed, Jesus succeeded. This illustrates a critical aspect of his saving mission, in a real time and place: he came to do what mortals like us cannot do on our own. We need a Substitute, and we have one in Jesus.

Gordon's Calvary/
Garden Tomb ◇

Fish
Gate

Sheep's Pool/
Pool of Bethesda

Struthion
Pool

Israel's Pool

Kidron Valley

Antonia
Fortress

Sheep
Gate

Gethsemane

Calvary ◇

Court of the
Israelites

Temple

Eastern
Gate

Tower's
Pool

Court of the
Women

Gennath
Gate

Court of the
Gentiles

Palace of
Herod Antipas

Royal Stoa

Huldah
Gates

Palace
of
Herod
the
Great

UPPER
CITY

Gihon
Spring

Mansion of the
High Priest

LOWER
CITY

Upper Room

Serpent's
Pool

Mount of
Olives

Essene
Gate

Water Gate

Siloam Pool

Hinnom Valley

N
W ✦ E
S

0   500 ft
0   150 m

······ Wall of Herod the Great
—— Wall added by Agrippa, after 41 AD
—— Wall built by Suleiman, 16th century AD

9

WALKING WITH JESUS
TO THE JERUSALEM TEMPLE

LIKE OUR WALK WITH JESUS into the wilderness, this one takes us to a place we have been before with Israel. At the Temple, Jesus faces a similar temptation and succeeds in the very spot that Israel had failed. By getting right what Israel got wrong, Jesus once again demonstrates his credentials as the Savior who redeems by being a substitute.

The walk to the Temple comes with a couple of surprises. The first is who leads the way. In a previous chapter, we saw the Holy Spirit leading Jesus into the wilderness. Even though we were entering a dangerous place, we felt a measure of comfort knowing that the leader had Jesus's best interest in mind. That is not the case this time, as the one leading this walk is the very tempter who sought to harm Jesus in the wilderness: "Then the devil took him to the holy city" (Matthew 4:5).

The next surprise is the destination of the walk. The devil is not leading Jesus to a more remote part of the wilderness, further isolating him from others. He leads Jesus to the Temple complex in the holy city of Jerusalem, a place full of people and activity.

Once we arrive, we walk up one set of stairs after the next until we reach the highest point of the worship center. From this dizzying elevation, the people going about their daily business look like ants scurrying below. They have not noticed us yet, but they certainly will if Jesus does what the devil urges him to do. "Throw yourself down," Satan says, "For it is written: 'He will command his angels concerning you, and they will lift you up in their hands, so that you will not strike your foot against a stone'" (Matthew 4:6).

Let's pause for a moment and think about where we are. That impacts our understanding of this temptation.

The Bible describes sacred space as a series of concentric circles. The closer we get to the center, the holier the ground on which we stand. The Father created the earth, so in one sense, our whole world is sacred space. But the Bible goes on to identify part of this created world—the Promised Land—as particularly holy. The Lord used this sacred space to further reveal himself to mortals and to bring the plan of salvation to life.

But within the Holy Land we have an even holier spot, Jerusalem, a city of the Lord's own choosing. At the time of Moses, God declared that he would identify one physical setting to which his people would come to worship, where he would meet them in a special way (Deuteronomy 12:4–6). In time, the Lord identified that location as Jerusalem: "For the LORD has chosen Zion, he has desired it for his dwelling, saying, 'This is my resting place forever and ever; here I will sit enthroned for I have desired it'" (Psalm 132:13–14).

We are not done yet—there is one smaller circle within the circle of Jerusalem, that is, the Temple itself. When Solomon dedicated the first Temple in Jerusalem, he acknowledged that the building could not contain the Lord—nevertheless, God was present in a special way, receiving the requests and worship of his people there (1 Kings 8:22–53).

All of this means that the Temple in Jerusalem is the most sacred space described in the Bible. If we understand that, we will appreciate how bold a move Satan is making when he tempts Jesus to sin at the innermost circle of sacred space, the very home of Jesus's Father.

Our understanding of the temptation also grows when we consider how this place looked in Jesus's day. At first, in the time of Solomon, the Temple was a single building constructed on the high point of Mount Moriah. But that picture of a single building on a hilltop no longer does justice to the sprawling complex that took shape at the time of Herod the Great. The main structure remains the focal point, but stretching in every direction from the Temple proper, we meet carefully crafted courtyards and monumental buildings. To walk into this Temple complex is to walk into one of the largest and most ornate worship facilities the world has ever seen.

The Temple itself is still perched on the top of a small hill. But the hill is no longer evident. To create level space around the main building, space on which people could gather and worship, Herod constructed a thirty-six-acre paved plaza with multiple courtyards. On three sides of this plaza, colonnaded porches invite worshipers to find respite from the sun or rain. And a stunning public building, the Royal Stoa, rises out of the south side of the plaza near the main entrances.

Getting to the plaza and beyond, to the highest part of the Temple complex, requires a climb. So, starting in Jerusalem's Central Valley, we walk with Jesus up a wide L-shaped stairway. Then we continue to an overlook that is part of the Royal Stoa, to a place from which the shofar (ram's horn) sounds to mark the start and close of Sabbath. This puts us about one-hundred-and-fifty feet above the valley. At the edge of this precipice, looking down on the busy shopping mall that fills the street below, the devil invites Jesus to take just one more step.

What is he up to? Gravity ensures that a fall would be fatal. But the devil's plan is not to kill Jesus—he wants to trick Jesus into seeking public recognition by an act of presumptive carelessness. Quoting the words of Psalm 91, the devil assures Jesus that he can afford to be a little careless, considering the protection provided by angels.

What is more, this is the house of Jesus's Father! We are all protective of our children, particularly in our own homes. We cover electrical outlets and guard stairways with devices meant to keep the young ones safe. The heavenly Father is not about to let Jesus fall to his death, and particularly not in his own house. The devil knows this, and urges Jesus to be careless. He can afford that here, particularly given what this moment could mean for him: Jesus can obtain kingly recognition without going to the cross. If he steps off the edge of the Temple and floats gently to earth before the eyes of those gathered in the market below, his political future is guaranteed. All it would take is a little presumption, a little carelessness. After all, this is the Temple of the Lord.

Wait just a minute! Those words sound familiar. We have heard this message before, and it was spoken in this same place.

In the time of Jeremiah, the devil tempted people to be careless in their behavior at the Temple in Jerusalem, to presume that no harm would come to them. Six hundred years earlier, in this same location, the prophet gave a sermon in which he listed all the sins God's people had committed. The list is as long as it is shocking: they had abused the socially vulnerable (orphans and widows), shed innocent blood, stolen, murdered, committed adultery, committed perjury, and worshiped pagan deities, including the infamous Baal (Jeremiah 7:5–6, 9). Jeremiah warned the people that this behavior had brought the Lord to the brink of action against them. The armies of the Babylonian empire were marching toward Jerusalem, and they were not interested in worship. They were on the way to destroy the city and the Lord's Temple.

And that was not even the worst of it. The biggest problem was that the devil had stirred presumption in God's people, convincing them to think carelessly about the Temple. We know this because Jeremiah urges the people to revisit their assumptions: "Do not trust in deceptive words and say, 'This is the temple of the Lord, the temple of the Lord, the temple of the Lord!'" (Jeremiah 7:4). In the people's minds, repentance was unnecessary because they were in the most sacred—and presumably, the safest—spot on earth. The terrible judgment about which Jeremiah warned could never happen here. This is the Temple of the Lord!

That is why the devil brings Jesus here. Back in the time of

Jeremiah, he had successfully made Israel sin in this same sacred space.

We can see the symmetry: the devil tempted Israelites to be careless with their spiritual life at the Temple in Jerusalem. And the devil did the same thing to Jesus, in the same place. But the next page of these stories could not be more different.

Israel continually insisted that no harm would come to them or to the Lord's house, right up to the moment that the Babylonian arrows began to fly. The Lord's own city was put under siege and the Temple itself was destroyed in 586 BC.

Jesus, standing in a rebuilt Temple, faces the same temptation. Will he fall victim to the careless presumption that had infected Israel? Will he take that step off the high point of the Temple at the devil's invitation? No! Jesus does not carelessly test his Father. His answer could not be more different than the one Israel, at the time of Jeremiah, had given in this place: "It is also written: 'Do not put the Lord your God to the test'" (Matthew 4:7).

Place again has brought together two stories widely separated in the pages of our Bible. The Temple in Jerusalem had changed in the six hundred years between these stories, but the devil's tactics had not. The tempter led Jesus to the very same location where Israel had been careless in their thinking about the Temple, confronting him with the same temptation. But in a complete reversal of what we had seen here before, Jesus met the temptation of Satan and won. As the saving substitute, Jesus succeeded at the Temple where Israel had failed.

We have walked with Jesus to four locations that are very different from one another—Egypt, the Jordan River, the wilderness, and the Temple in Jerusalem. But they have one thing in common: each of these places hosted an important experience in the lives of God's chosen people in the time of the Old Testament.

Centuries later, the gospel authors invite us to walk with Jesus to these very locations. And in them, Jesus experiences situations that parallel those of Israel. The parallels are not accidental—they teach us that Jesus is fully capable of encountering everything another human being might. In doing so, he has passed the first test of being a substitute.

But if that is all Jesus was, he falls short of what we need. As much as I might appreciate another human offering himself or herself as my substitute before the Father, it would be meaningless unless that person could offer obedience in place of my disobedience. That is where Jesus is different, and when we walk with Jesus to the wilderness and to the Temple in Jerusalem, we see that difference.

This Son of Man is also the Son of God, capable of living a life of obedience that we cannot. We have seen Jesus put himself in the same physical settings that had witnessed a defeat of God's people of the past. But in those places where Israel failed, Jesus succeeded.

Here is just the kind of substitute we need. "For we do not have a high priest who is unable to empathize with our weaknesses, but we have one who has been tempted in every way, just as we are—yet he did not sin" (Hebrews 4:15).

1. When have you either been a substitute or benefited from someone taking your place? How do those experiences shed light on what a substitute is?

2. How do stories like the ones we have studied make the role of Jesus as our substitute more real and clear? What is the impact of having so many of these stories in the Gospels?

3. Where in the Bible have you seen Jesus encountering something in life in life that matches an experience you have had? How does that shape your personal relationship with him?

4. Recognizing that wilderness is not just a place but a season of life, how has the devil tempted you in the wilderness?

5. How have these walks with Jesus brought you a sense of peace?

PART THREE

Jesus, Geography, and Pagan Land Claims

OUR NEXT THREE DESTINATIONS HAVE a pagan past. These are places in which Satan laid claim to space that rightfully belonged to the Lord.

The devil's apparent success in such places leaves us with questions: Are there places where the Lord is *not* sovereign over evil? Are there places where pagan land claims are valid? These are important questions, which will be answered when we walk with Jesus to these locations.

The walks take us to places we might otherwise avoid, places hosting and celebrating ungodly power and influence. We will walk with Jesus to Caesarea Philippi, a pagan sanctuary of the New Testament era that is adjacent to Dan, a pagan sanctuary in Old Testament times. We will walk with Jesus to the region of Tyre and Sidon, where he healed the daughter of a Canaanite woman in the neighborhood that Baal-worshiping Jezebel called home. Finally, we will walk with Jesus to the Temple in Jerusalem. Yes, even this holy place had its unholy moments when a pagan mind-set controlled it.

But Jesus takes us to locations with a pagan backstory to demonstrate that Satan's claims have no substance or merit. Where paganism makes a haughty display of power, Jesus illustrates the truth of his own words, "In this world you will have trouble. But take heart! I have overcome the world" (John 16:33).

Make no mistake: this *is* our Father's world. But until Jesus's second coming, we walk in a world that still has pagan portals, sanctuaries to Satan. How should we think about them? How can we overcome their influence? We will find the answers when we walk along the road with Jesus.

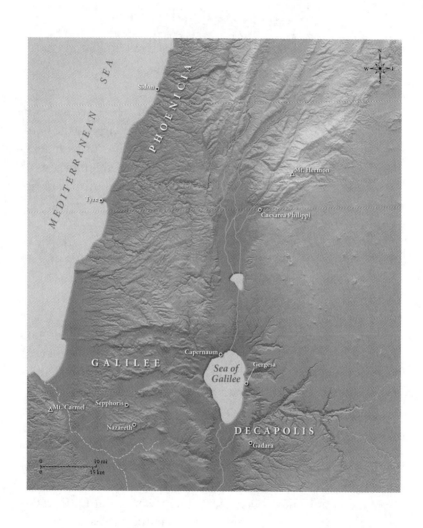

10

WALKING WITH JESUS
TO CAESAREA PHILIPPI

WE CAN EXPECT CONFRONTATION WHEN we make our way with Jesus to "the region of Caesarea Philippi" (Matthew 16:13). Here, at the base of Mount Hermon, the pagan world has staked a land claim, first at the city of Dan and then at the adjacent city of Caesarea Philippi. Both sites are impressive in size and appearance. Both assert that the pagan world has unimaginable power and influence. Jesus comes to this region to debunk these lofty claims.

Caesarea Philippi has a political past that meshes with its pagan claims. Its name outlines the backstory: *Caesar* Augustus, emperor of Rome, gave this area to Herod the Great. After Herod's death, his son *Philip* received this region and made the city at the base of Mount Hermon its regional capital. To create the city's name, Philip added his own name to that of Caesar Augustus.

Both Herod and Philip further honored Caesar with a large public building, an ornate, marble temple designed for worshiping the emperor as divine. But this pagan architecture was not the first at Caesarea. Pagan sanctuaries often appear in places with an otherworldly, physical appearance, and that is certainly the case here.

Philip constructed his city in front of the southernmost ridge of Mount Hermon, a sheer, 131-foot cliff that in the sun glows softly with a variety of colors. At the base of this cliff, a hole 66 feet wide and 49 feet tall forms an opening in the rock face; in Jesus's time, water gushed from this deep cave at over 5,000 gallons per second. To this day, there is a haunting look to the place.

If you can imagine a pagan mind-set for a moment, you will

see why this site gave birth to a sanctuary to false gods. For those who do not recognize the Father as creator, the mysteries of creation become gods. Things you cannot explain (such as rainfall) and things you want to guarantee (such as the fertility of your livestock) become associated with deities. And because these deities are thought to perform better in some locations rather than others, you look for places to worship them where their influence is most apparent.

That is why this cliff face and cave were chosen. The beautiful location, so rich in natural resources, became the worship site for Pan, the half-man-half-goat deity of nature and shepherds. It was established about 220 BC. Later during the time of Herod the Great, an adjacent temple was built in front of the cave in honor of the Roman emperor Augustus. By the start of the first century, pagan rituals were ongoing at both locations.

Jesus brought the disciples into this place, far from the Jewish cultural orbit in which we usually find him, because it would help him teach some important lessons. He needed to return to Jerusalem one last time; Jesus told the disciples this trip would end in his suffering, death, and resurrection (Matthew 16:21). In this moment, the disciples needed to know that Jesus was up to this challenge—and they needed to know they were up for the challenge of advancing the Kingdom of God after their leader's departure.

So Jesus brings them to this pagan place for a conversation about his identity and capability. Western cultures tend to see these as two different, descriptive qualities. But in the world of Jesus, they are conjoined: who you are defines what you are able to do. He begins with a question about identity that doubles as a question about capability. "'But what about you?' he asked. 'Who do you say I am?'" (Matthew 16:15). Reading between the lines, we see that Jesus is asking, *Do you think I am up to the task that lies ahead in Jerusalem?*

The timing makes this a critical question, and the place will clarify the answer. Here, before the gods of the pagan world, Jesus wants the disciples (and us) to reflect on how he compares with the competition, the deities that had laid claim to this mountain cliff. Simon Peter, rarely shy to speak, answers Jesus's question by saying, "You are the Messiah, the Son of the living God" (Matthew 16:16).

In one brief sentence, Peter confesses the uniqueness of Jesus and a power that exceeds that of every deity at Caesarea Philippi. This God is "living"; the other deities that people claimed to be alive are not. Jesus is the Messiah, the Son of God. This is someone who can go to Jerusalem and accomplish just what he said he would.

But what of Peter and the others? The conversation turns from Jesus's identity and capabilities to that of Peter as a representative of the disciples. Peter's confession is so powerful and so important to the future well-being of the church that Jesus uses a visual from Caesarea Philippi to make it stick. "Blessed are you, Simon son of Jonah," Jesus says, "for this was not revealed to you by flesh and blood but by my Father in heaven. And I tell you that you are Peter, and on this rock I will build my church" (Matthew 16:17–18).

Peter comes from the Greek word for "rock." And as the disciples look up at the biggest rock cliff in the region, this one hovering above Caesarea Philippi, he invites them to anchor the lesson in the view. The lower ridge of this "rock" was one on which the pagan world had built its understanding and hope. However, it is not the rock at Caesarea Philippi but "this rock"—the rock of Peter's confession—on which the church would be built. Those who make such a confession are like Mount Hermon, the tallest and most dominant mountain in the entire region.

And what about the pagan world that had laid claim to this cliff? Would it be successful in defeating the growth of God's Kingdom? Jesus turns the disciples' eyes toward the yawning cave at the base of the cliff. The church father Eusebius tells us the Romans believed this eerie opening was the gateway to Hades, the underworld. With that cave and the pagan sanctuaries that flanked it in view, Jesus declares the certainty of the church's future: "the gates of Hades will not overcome it" (Matthew 16:18).

As we integrate the view at Caesarea Philippi with the powerful teaching of Jesus, we get that feeling again—the feeling that we have been here before. And, basically, we have. We have not been to Caesarea Philippi but, as Old Testament readers, we have spent considerable time at Dan. That is also a city built at the base of Mount Hermon, a mere two miles west. These cities share not just a general location but an affection for pagan practice.

Dan's story began with the dividing of Israel into two kingdoms. Following the death of Solomon, the nation split into a northern kingdom (called Israel) and a southern kingdom (called Judah). The Promised Land now housed two distinct political entities with separate capital cities and separate kings. Although the Lord sponsored this political division, he insisted that there be just one religious center—Jerusalem—which would focus the two kingdoms on their shared spiritual assignment.

Jeroboam, the first ruler of the northern kingdom, saw the Lord's plan as harmful to his own political future and sought to upend it. "Jeroboam thought to himself, 'The kingdom will now likely revert to the house of David. If these people go up to offer sacrifices at the temple of the LORD in Jerusalem, they will again give their allegiance to their lord, Rehoboam king of Judah. They will kill me and return to King Rehoboam'" (1 Kings 12:26–27). So Jeroboam set about creating a religious system separate from that in Jerusalem.

Jeroboam had subjects with different religious backgrounds, some of them Canaanites with a history of worshiping Baal, others descendants of Abraham, whose family had worshiped the Lord who brought them out of Egypt. Consequently, Jeroboam designed a new religion that combined elements from both groups.

The golden calf image was familiar to the worshipers of Baal. The Exodus from Egypt was an event linked to the Lord. Jeroboam made a pair of gold calves and urged his subjects to fall in behind him and his new national religion: "It is too much for you to go up to Jerusalem. Here are your gods, Israel, who brought you up out of Egypt" (1 Kings 12:28). Jeroboam established two worship complexes for this hybrid religion, one at the south end of his kingdom, Bethel, and the other in the far north, at Dan. "And this thing became a sin; the people came to worship the one at Bethel and went as far as Dan to worship the other" (1 Kings 12:30).

This spiritual perversion so corrupted the northern kingdom that it was referred to again and again by the Old Testament authors (1 Kings 13:34; 16:26; 22:52; 2 Kings 17:21; 23:15). The base of Mount Hermon became intimately linked to this paganism that endured throughout the entire history of the northern kingdom of Israel.

For centuries, the pagan world had defiantly laid claim to this land, using it to champion an alternative spiritual reality—the belief in many gods. This pagan perspective taught that the Lord was not fully sovereign over the Promised Land, and the idea lingered over the landscape into the time of Jesus. So he came here to put an end to the charade before walking to Jerusalem one last time.

This was his Father's world. It did not belong to the golden calves of Dan, the nature deity Pan, or the emperor of Rome. Jesus took the disciples to the region of Caesarea Philippi and got in the face of its pagan claims, asserting in no uncertain terms that *he* was the Son of God. There were no other gods before him, and he alone had the ability to go to Jerusalem and win salvation for the world. And it was his followers, not those of the pagan deities at Caesarea, who would endure like Mount Hermon.

Jesus came to the region of Caesarea Philippi to reclaim a land the pagan world had claimed as its own.

11

WALKING WITH JESUS TO THE REGION OF TYRE AND SIDON

WHEN I WAS IN COLLEGE, I spent my summers working on the grounds crew of a resort. Every morning, I began my day with a walk around the parking lot to pick up garbage. During one of those walks, I met a professional basketball player I admired. In an arena with thousands of other spectators, I had watched the man play from a distance—but I never expected to shake his hand in a parking lot as I was picking up trash. Years later, while boarding an airliner for a business trip, I had a similar experience when the captain addressed me by name as I stepped aboard. He had been a flight student of mine, but I hadn't seen him for a decade.

We feel the same kind of surprise in a story from Jesus's life, as we meet a woman of great faith where we wouldn't expect to find her—in the region that gave us Jezebel.

This story, in Matthew 15:21–28, evolves very differently than most of our accounts about Jesus. An unnamed woman approaches him using the title "Son of David," demonstrating that she has some familiarity with the Old Testament and its expectation of a coming Messiah. This woman comes to Jesus with a desperate plea: her daughter is possessed by a demon and suffering horribly, and she wants Jesus to help.

As readers of the Gospels, we have seen Jesus react to these situations before—so we expect that he will quickly provide a healing. But his reaction is far from ordinary. At first, Jesus ignores the woman. Then the disciples grow tired of her persistence and urge Jesus to send her away.

Jesus doesn't rebuke them. Instead, he turns to the woman

and tells her that she does not belong to the right ethnic group! "I was sent only to the lost sheep of Israel," he says (Matthew 15:24).

Undeterred, the woman kneels before Jesus, pleading again for his help. Jesus again deflects her request, likening her posture to a dog begging for food at the dinner table: "It is not right to take the children's bread and toss it to the dogs" (Matthew 21:26).

How much more rejection and insult can this woman endure? Desperate to get help for her daughter, she tries one more time. She humbly acknowledges her dog-like status, echoing Jesus's language but sustaining her request. "Even the dogs," she says, "eat the crumbs that fall from their master's table" (Matthew 21:27).

What an incredible faith! And that appears to be Jesus's point in delaying the assistance she requests. This woman's faith is so powerful that it pushes through all the insults and rejection without surrendering. This bold and persistent faith is one that Jesus wants the disciples to see. The delay in honoring the woman's request for her daughter's healing allows the nature of her faith to come into the light.

Now let's add the setting for this amazing faith. It is found in an unexpected place, the region of Tyre and Sidon.

In telling this story, Matthew states that Jesus did not just "go out" but that he "withdrew" to this region. That is because this walk takes us completely out of the Promised Land. The destination is a region that the Greeks called Phoenicia. But at the time of Jesus, this area had been incorporated into the larger Roman district of Syria. Consequently, the woman who comes to Jesus could be identified as a Phoenician or as a Syrian, but Matthew elects to call her a "Canaanite," the label the indigenous people used when referring to themselves.

This label reminds us that the woman lived outside the land where the Old Testament was read and preached. Yet here in this Gentile place, pagan country in both the Old and New Testament eras, we find a woman who gets closer to the gold standard of faith than most people in the Promised Land. That is why Jesus invites us to walk into this place with him. He wants to show us that this kind of faith can exist even in a pagan locale.

The lesson stands out even more starkly when we recall that we have been in this region before—it is a place with a long pagan backstory. The nameless woman from the region of Tyre and Sidon calls to mind a woman with an all-too-familiar name, Jezebel. She may be the most infamous pagan woman we meet in the Old Testament.

Jezebel came from Sidon, partner city to Tyre, in the region the Old Testament calls Phoenicia. Her story crossed paths with that of God's people due to an economic enhancement plan developed by Omri and Ahab. These two kings of the northern kingdom, father and son, respectively, saw the strength in the Phoenician economy. So they sought a partnership that would bring some of this wealth into their own country of Israel.

Tyre and Sidon had become an economic powerhouse. As cities on the coast of the Mediterranean Sea, they enjoyed natural deep-water harbors. To their east, the mountains offered a ready supply of high-quality timber—the cedars of Lebanon—prime shipbuilding material. Thus, the geography of Phoenicia destined it to develop a strong maritime culture. The Phoenicians' cargo ships and sailing skills took them to the far corners of the Mediterranean world.

Beyond ships and sailors, Tyre and Sidon also provided the world with a distribution hub through which international goods flowed to and from the trading colonies they established around the Mediterranean basin. For a more detailed picture, read Ezekiel 27—here you will learn about the ships, shipwrights, linens, precious metals, chariots, horses, ivory, aromatics, and agricultural goods that fueled these cities' success. Location, maritime skills, and a vast trade network combined to drive Phoenicia's economic engine, which then lured the attention of Omri and Ahab.

These Israelite kings wanted to divert the overland movement of international trade goods through their own country. Prior to this time, goods from the lands south and east of Israel traveled to market through Damascus, up the King's Highway that ran east of the Jordan River—that is, outside Israel. Omri planned to divert those goods west of the Jordan, moving them through his country and then on to the ports of Tyre and Sidon for distribution. Both Israel and Phoenicia stood to benefit from this plan.

To seal the business deal, Omri arranged a marriage between Ahab, his son, and Jezebel. She is called the "daughter of Ethbaal king of the Sidonians" (1 Kings 16:31).

Notice the divine name that forms part of her father's name. Jezebel's family members were ardent Baal worshipers. When she packed up her belongings to move to Israel, she brought along her passion for Baal. In time, Ahab and Jezebel together would bind that pagan mind-set to the northern kingdom of Israel. The Bible does not comment directly on his motivation. But it would seem that Ahab went along because he believed that the economic success of Phoenicia was, in part, connected to the blessing of this pagan deity.

In Jezebel's homeland, the king was also the high priest who directed religious matters. That was not to be the case among God's people, who were served by a separate priesthood. But the Lord's concerns were not Ahab and Jezebel's, so this couple built a temple to Baal in the capital city of Samaria (1 Kings 16:32). They put pagan priests on the payroll of their kingdom (1 Kings 18:19). When the Lord sent prophets to challenge the worship of Baal, Jezebel had them killed (1 Kings 18:4). She also saw to the execution of Naboth who—in obedience to God's laws—declined to sell his family's vineyard to Ahab (1 Kings 21:1–14). In the end, thanks to Jezebel, Ahab receives the worst spiritual evaluation of any of the kings of God's people: "There was never anyone like Ahab, who sold himself to do evil in the eyes of the Lord, urged on by Jezebel his wife" (1 Kings 21:25).

This horrible backstory makes us cringe and creates expectations about the kind of people who live in region of Tyre and Sidon. When we walk with Jesus to this region, we expect to meet paganism. We expect to find Satan having his way among people who have rejected the Almighty.

Now, as the nameless woman approaches Jesus, the story of Jezebel comes to mind and we expect him to react to her like he might react to Jezebel. The story starts to deliver on those expectations—we meet a woman whose daughter is possessed by a demon. We see Jesus dismissing her as a non-Jew, unworthy of attention. We even see Jesus likening her to a dog, recalling the animals that devoured Jezebel and kept her from having an honorable burial (1 Kings 21:23; 2 Kings 9:10, 36).

Expectations met. Let's go back to the Promised Land.

But wait one minute. This nameless woman is no Jezebel. Although there are plenty of pagan deities from whom she could seek help, she comes to Jesus. She does not invoke the name of a false god like Baal, but pleads for help from the "Son of David," an Old Testament title used for the promised Messiah. When she faces rejection and insult, this woman does not give up but relentlessly pursues Jesus with a faith and hope unlike any we have seen in the Promised Land. Certainly, this is no Jezebel.

And that is why Jesus wanted us to walk with him, out of the Promised Land and into a place so steeped in a pagan past. He brought us here to show this woman's faith as an example of what the Holy Spirit can do in a person's heart—even in a place with a strong pagan heritage.

What a lesson that teaches. We tend to dismiss pagan places as hopeless, unredeemable. We can write them off, together with their residents, as outside the Kingdom of God. We may even dismiss their misery as a deserved retribution. But this story offers a helpful corrective to that thinking.

For sure, we meet people of faith—and sometimes exemplary faith—in holy places. We expect to meet them in our churches and Bible studies. But what about the places steeped in paganism? Are these places outside the Lord's reach? No, God has a rightful claim on such places and their people. This walk with Jesus to the region of Tyre and Sidon makes that clear.

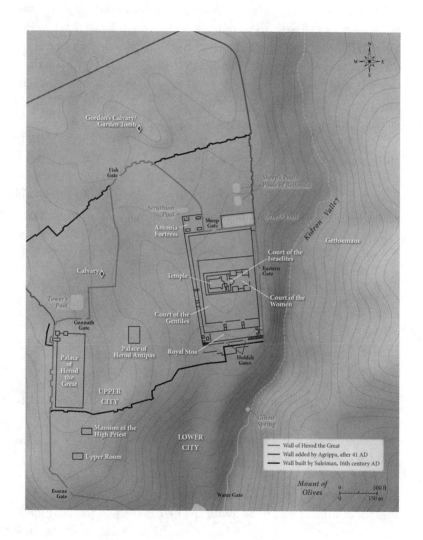

Gordon's Calvary/
Garden Tomb

Fish
Gate

Sheep's Pool/
Pools of Bethesda

Struthion
Pool

Israel's Pool

Sheep
Gate

Antonia
Fortress

Kidron Valley

Gethsemane

Court of the
Israelites

Calvary

Temple

Eastern
Gate

Tower's
Pool

Court of the
Women

Court of the
Gentiles

Gennath
Gate

Palace of
Herod Antipas

Royal Stoa

Huldah
Gates

Palace
of
Herod
the
Great

UPPER
CITY

Gihon
Spring

Mansion of the
High Priest

LOWER
CITY

Upper Room

Wall of Herod the Great
Wall added by Agrippa, after 41 AD
Wall built by Suleiman, 16th century AD

Essene
Gate

Water Gate

Mount of
Olives

0   500 ft
0   150 m

12

WALKING WITH JESUS
TO THE JERUSALEM TEMPLE

THE DESTINATION OF THIS WALK seems to be misplaced in this part of the book. We have been focusing on locales associated with pagan land claims—places like Phoenicia and the base of Mount Hermon. But the Temple is different. It is a holy place, the site in which the Lord made his presence known in a special way, a location to focus on holy thoughts and holy living.

That is what the Temple in Jerusalem *should* be. But on two occasions, one from the lifetime of Nehemiah and the other from the days of Jesus, we find this sacred space infiltrated and controlled by a pagan mind-set. This walk with Jesus to the Temple reminds us that we cannot let our guard down, even in places we consider sacred. And this walk teaches us what to do when a sacred space is counterclaimed by paganism. There is no room for compromise, only cleansing.

This walk toward the Temple takes place during Passover (Matthew 21:1–13). Passover was one of the high holy days on which the Lord asked his chosen people to come to the holy city and spend time at his holy Temple. This was not a vacation but a spiritual journey. Ordinary concerns of life like growing grain, raising livestock, and repairing the house gave way to a time of focus on the Lord and one's relationship with him.

The Passover ritual required worshipers to have an animal for sacrifice, so each pilgrim needed either to bring one from home or secure one for themselves in Jerusalem (Deuteronomy 16:1–4). Beyond that, Passover was often the festival during which Israelite males paid the required half-shekel Temple tax, money used for the upkeep of the facility and maintenance of the worship conducted there (Exodus 30:11–16; 2 Chronicles 24:8–12). That collection began the month before Passover, but payments were often made during this trip to Jerusalem.

That is why this walk with Jesus, on the way to worship, takes us past animal markets and money exchanges. For those who had not brought an animal from home or whose animal was found to have a defect that made it unusable in this religious rite, vendors were happy to provide options, at a cost. Those shopping in the Temple markets or paying their taxes carried a wide variety of coins that were circulating in the first century, but Temple officials accepted only Tyrian shekels, coins minted with higher quality silver and made with a more consistent amount of metal. Given that this was the only acceptable coin in the Temple markets, money exchange stations arose to serve the worshipers. Of course, there was a fee charged for this service.

We expect to walk quickly past this noisy, smelly market space. But Jesus stops and starts behaving in ways that are, frankly, shocking. "He made a whip out of cords, and drove all from the temple courts, both sheep and cattle; he scattered the coins of the money changers and overturned their tables. To those who sold doves he said, 'Get these out of here! Stop turning my Father's house into a market!'" (John 2:15–16).

This is not the mild-mannered Jesus that many expect, but the incensed Son of God. Something about these markets has touched a nerve with him. There is nothing wrong with providing a service for worshipers coming to Jerusalem, but Jesus's passionate response, angry words, and aggressive actions are fueled by the location of the markets and the attitude of those who run them.

Let's start with the location. These markets were primarily situated in the Royal Stoa and in the courtyard just to its north. The Royal Stoa was a monumental building on the south side of the sprawling Temple complex, impressing visitors by its size, style, and decoration. It was a long building with three aisles separated by four sets of columns. The entire structure was more than 600 feet long and more than 70 feet wide. The roof of the side aisles was 49 feet tall and the roof of the central aisle more than twice that height. But it appeared to be even taller because it was built on top of the Temple Mount, some 200 feet above the valley systems surrounding it. This art-filled structure would be impressive by today's standards, so just imagine the visual impact on those who came from the villages of Israel, people who lived in small one- or two-story homes and rarely encountered public buildings of any kind. The Royal Stoa provided one of the grand entrances into the Temple.

The Sadducees who run the markets are also in charge of the Temple. These aristocratic priests operate the place like a business, seemingly more interested in making money than improving the well-being of people's souls. The Sadducees view people coming to worship as "customers" and, for the best sales, set up their markets in the high-traffic areas of the Temple grounds. This completely changes the worship experience, as your attention is not drawn to the magnificent entrance to the Father's house but to the sounds, sights, and smell of livestock.

Add to that the questionable way in which the markets are run. The aristocratic priests are the inspectors who determine if an animal meets the quality standards for sacrifice. When they "find" a problem with the animal you brought from home, they are quick to point you to the preapproved animals for sale in the Royal Stoa. And when you produce coins that are not considered worthy currency for use in the market, they point you to the moneychangers, who are glad to make the exchange for a fee.

These pagan attitudes and actions of the aristocratic priests should have no place in Jerusalem, much less at the very entry of the Temple. The worship experience of God's people is tarnished from the very start. And that is why Jesus responds in such a forceful fashion. This is his Father's house, and those running the

Temple markets have turned the place into something less than it should be. So Jesus creates a stir by driving out the animals and overturning tables.

There it is again, a sense of déjà vu. This story reminds us of another time when the Temple had become something less than it should be—and furniture started flying. That happened at the time of Nehemiah.

This story is less well known than the one of Jesus's cleansing of the Temple, but the two belong together. Nehemiah's is also a Jerusalem Temple story, in the time following the tragic exile of God's people to Babylon. This event was a product of Israel's spiritual carelessness—they had failed to be the people the Lord had called them to be, worshiping other gods and interfering with God's plan to save the world. That is serious stuff, so the Lord allowed the soldiers of Babylon to enter the Promised Land and defeat the armies defending Jerusalem. The city was ransacked and God's people deported from the Promised Land to live in exile for seventy years. Almost unthinkably, the Temple itself was demolished.

Following the exile, Nehemiah—together with Ezra the priest—led the people returning from Babylon to rebuild the Temple, as well as the faithfulness of God's people.

Against this backdrop, a priest named Eliashib did something at the Temple that required strong redress. This story, found in Nehemiah 13:4–9, occurred long before the Temple complex was renovated by Herod the Great, so there was no Royal Stoa as in Jesus's day. But there were storerooms, used to house the grain offerings, incense, and temple articles as well as the tithes of grain, new wine, and olive oil that supplied the needs of the temple workers. By all accounts, this was sacred space set apart for divine service.

Incredibly, Eliashib had emptied one of these storerooms so that a man named Tobiah could store his personal household items. This was bad enough for anyone, but it is particularly egregious in the case of Tobiah. He was an Ammonite who had acquired a high political position, becoming a regional administrator on behalf of Persia. In that capacity, Tobiah had vigorously opposed the rebuilding of the Temple (Nehemiah 2:10, 19; 4:3, 7–8; 6:16–17).

Ironically, now that the Temple was rebuilt, Tobiah wanted space within it to use as a personal residence while he was in town. Put all of that together: this was a non-Israelite, a pagan, a foreign leader who had worked to prevent the building of the Lord's Temple. But at Tobiah's request, Eliashib removed sacred material from a Temple storeroom, giving the space to Tobiah for his use.

Eliashib may have seen this as a shrewd political move, but Nehemiah viewed it differently. When he heard about this after being away from Jerusalem, Nehemiah responded quickly. "Here I learned about the evil thing Eliashib had done in providing Tobiah a room in the courts of the house of God. I was greatly displeased and threw all Tobiah's household goods out of the room. I gave orders to purify the rooms, and then I put back into them the equipment of the house of God, with the grain offerings and the incense" (Nehemiah 13:7–9).

The parallels between this story and that of Jesus are striking. Both are set in the Lord's house in Jerusalem. In both cases, pagan influence had entered the physical grounds of the Temple, disrupting the role it was to play in the lives of God's people. In both cases, the abuse was sponsored by the priestly leadership. And in both cases, the corrective action was not a discussion or a compromise but the aggressive removal of the offensive things from sacred space.

These stories, occurring at different times in the same location, combine to teach two important lessons. First, pagan influences can enter even sacred space. Today, we have sacred spaces in our lives, places either in our homes or in our churches where we leave mundane things behind and focus on the Lord and our relationship with him. But Satan seems to take great delight in compromising these sacred spaces and claiming them as his own—we need to stay alert for this kind of invasion.

Second, these stories illustrate how we should respond when we see a pagan influence entering our sacred space. This is no trifling matter; there is no room for compromise. When a pagan influence is found in our Christian school, our study group, or our church, we need to throw it out. I am not advocating violence, of course—that would not be appropriate. But the way in which Nehemiah and Jesus responded to this invasion of the Lord's Temple shows that nothing short of aggressive action is warranted.

Pagan influence has no place in sacred space. When we find it, there is only one response: not compromise but cleansing.

In this part of the book, we have walked with Jesus to places on which the pagan world made a claim. First, we traveled to the rocky base of Mount Hermon. In Old Testament times, this land was claimed by the hybrid worship established by Jeroboam at Dan; in Jesus's day at Caesarea Philippi, the area was claimed by either the worship of Pan or the Roman emperor. Jesus took us to this location to make a counterclaim, asserting that this space belonged to his Father and that he is stronger than the pagan deities who called this place home. The real rock on which the church is built is the confession of Jesus as Messiah.

Our second walk took us out of the Promised Land to the region of Tyre and Sidon. This was also land claimed by the pagan world, most notably by those who worshiped Baal. We would expect to meet people like Jezebel here, but were taken aback by the nameless woman who sought healing for her demon-possessed daughter. Her exemplary faith demonstrated that even the homeland of Jezebel did not belong to Satan.

And our last walk was to the Temple in Jerusalem. Here we learned through two stories, one from the life of Jesus and the other from the life of Nehemiah, that even sacred spaces can be infiltrated by Satan. In these geographically paired stories, we are encouraged to keep our guard up even when we are in sacred space. And when we find a pagan influence there, our response should be as quick and decisive as those of Jesus and Nehemiah. Pagan influence in sacred space needs to be met with cleansing.

1. Where in your world do you see paganism laying claim to physical space? How does Satan use places like that to advance his reach and influence?

2. How did the scenery and history of Caesarea Philippi support Jesus's discussion about his identity and capability (as

well as the disciples'), and help to defeat the pagan claim on this land?

3. Why is it surprising to meet a woman of such remarkable faith in the region of Tyre and Sidon? How did her story change your view of that place?

4. Have you ever found a powerful testimony of faith in a place you had not expected? Are examples of faith in pagan places more or less powerful than a faith witness in sacred space? Why?

5. Have you ever seen pagan influence infiltrate the life of your church? How did you respond? What does the story of Jesus cleansing the Temple teach about how best to respond when meeting pagan influence in your sacred places?

PART FOUR

Jesus, Geography, and Divine Titles

"WHAT DO YOU DO FOR a living?" This is one of the first questions I ask when getting to know someone. Of course, there is more to people than what they do for a living. But the answers to this question deepen my understanding of who they are, what native skills they possess, and how they think about the human experience.

As Jesus walked from place to place, he continually met new people, and they needed to understand who he was, what skills he had, and how he viewed the human experience. So one way Jesus introduced himself to others was by using his "professional titles." But he rarely, in direct speech, assigned one of those titles to himself. In other words, Jesus did not say things like, "I am a prophet" or "I am a king."

He did, however, go to very specific places associated with those titles in the Old Testament era. Using those settings as a backdrop, Jesus said and did things that led others to link him with the titles. At a well outside the Samaritan village of Sychar, he received the title Messiah. On Mount Moreh, the title Prophet. Walking down the Mount of Olives toward the Gihon Spring, he received the title King. And as he sat above the Kidron Valley, he linked himself to the title of Judge.

In this part of the book, we will walk with Jesus to these places, seeing how he used geography to connect himself with divine titles. And just as those who first traveled with Jesus to these locations had "*aha* moments," we can expect that our walks will lead to a gratifying sense of discovery. They will confirm that Jesus is our Messiah, our Prophet, our King, and our Judge.

13

WALKING WITH JESUS TO SYCHAR

THE APOSTLE JOHN DESCRIBES MANY walks he took with Jesus, but only once does he characterize the itinerary with language like this: "Now he *had to* go through Samaria" (John 4:4, emphasis mine).

This unique description sends us in search of answers. Why does John introduce the trip with this strong language? Why was it necessary for Jesus to travel through Samaria to Sychar? Did Jesus "have to go through Samaria" because it was the only route available to him?

Let's first consider his larger plan. Jesus was traveling from Judea in the south to the district of Galilee farther north (John 4:3). When we consider the ancient road systems, Jesus had other options for making this trip, options that did not require him to journey through Samaria. So why did he choose this route?

Jesus unveils the answer when he stops at a well outside the village of Sychar. Here he does something that he rarely ever did, verbally acknowledging that he was the Messiah. It is a declaration that has to be made here.

This story comes from the early chapters of John's gospel, where the apostle introduces us to Jesus by inviting us to watch the ways in which he introduced himself to others. To say the least, these introductions did not always go well. Jesus introduced himself to the religious leadership by overturning tables and scattering animals in the Temple markets (2:13–17). The Temple leadership was not impressed. Jesus introduced himself to Nicodemus, a Jewish scholar, by describing the need to be "born again." Nicodemus could not make sense of it (3:1–10). Even John the Baptist's disciples appeared confused over Jesus's identity and relationship to John

(3:25–26). What is particularly noteworthy (and ironic) is that all these stories are from Judea. This is the part of the Promised Land that prided itself on having a more sophisticated understanding of all things religious. By the end of chapter three, we wonder if anyone is going to understand who Jesus is.

Our expectations run particularly low when we look at the geography that opens the next chapter. Jesus has left Judea and stopped at Sychar, a village within the Roman district of Samaria, part of the Promised Land given to Joseph's extended family. In the eighth century before Christ, the Israelites who lived in this region rejected the truth the Lord had revealed to them, adopting the religious views of the cultures around them. They came to believe that there were many legitimate gods rather than just one. As a result, the Lord allowed the Assyrian empire to invade and conquer the land, exporting most of the Jewish locals and importing Gentiles from other conquered regions. In the end, this area became the home of an ethnically mixed and religiously blended people who got some things right but many more wrong when it came to worship of the one true God.

As the Old Testament described it, "Even while these people were worshiping the Lord, they were serving their idols. To this day their children and grandchildren continue to do as their ancestors did" (2 Kings 17:41). And this remained the case into the New Testament era, when residents of this Roman district were known as "Samaritans." If the people of Judea struggled to understand who Jesus was, what could we expect here in Samaria, a place famously unorthodox in its beliefs?

It is noon by the time we reach the well outside Sychar. Jesus is tired and thirsty, so he sits down near the well that serves the village. When a Samaritan woman comes to draw water, he asks her for a drink.

This marks the start of one of the most important conversations of Jesus's earthly ministry. Let's review the scene as described in John 4:4–26:

Now [Jesus] had to go through Samaria. So he came to a town in Samaria called Sychar, near the plot of ground Jacob had given to his son Joseph. Jacob's well was there, and Jesus, tired as he was from the journey, sat down by the well. It was about noon.

When a Samaritan woman came to draw water, Jesus said to her, "Will you give me a drink?" (His disciples had gone into the town to buy food.)

The Samaritan woman said to him, "You are a Jew and I am a Samaritan woman. How can you ask me for a drink?" (For Jews do not associate with Samaritans.)

Jesus answered her, "If you knew the gift of God and who it is that asks you for a drink, you would have asked him and he would have given you living water."

"Sir," the woman said, "you have nothing to draw with and the well is deep. Where can you get this living water? Are you greater than our father Jacob, who gave us the well and drank from it himself, as did also his sons and his livestock?"

Jesus answered, "Everyone who drinks this water will be thirsty again, but whoever drinks the water I give them will never thirst. Indeed, the water I give them will become in them a spring of water welling up to eternal life."

The woman said to him, "Sir, give me this water so that I won't get thirsty and have to keep coming here to draw water."

He told her, "Go, call your husband and come back."

"I have no husband," she replied.

Jesus said to her, "You are right when you say you have no husband. The fact is, you have had five husbands, and the man you now have is not your husband. What you have just said is quite true."

"Sir," the woman said, "I can see that you are a prophet. Our ancestors worshiped on this mountain, but you Jews claim that the place where we must worship is in Jerusalem."

"Woman," Jesus replied, "believe me, a time is coming when you will worship the Father neither on this mountain nor in Jerusalem. You Samaritans worship what you do not know; we worship what we do know, for salvation is from the Jews. Yet a time is coming and has now come when the true worshipers will worship the Father in the Spirit and in truth, for they are the kind of worshipers the Father seeks. God is spirit, and his worshipers must worship in the Spirit and in truth."

The woman said, "I know that Messiah" (called Christ) "is coming. When he comes, he will explain everything to us."

Then Jesus declared, "I, the one speaking to you—I am he."

Reflecting the tensions that existed between Samaritans and Jews, the woman deflects Jesus's request for a drink (4:9). This is when the conversation turns theological.

Jesus speaks of giving the woman "living water" (John 4:10), but she doesn't grasp the reference. In the prophetic books of the Old Testament, water is mentioned as a metaphor for God, His Word, and the message of salvation (Isaiah 12:3; 49:10; 55:1–3, 10–11; Jeremiah 2:13). If this woman knew that literature, she would have been able to understand the direction in which Jesus was taking the conversation. But since Samaritans recognize only the first five books of the Old Testament as their written authority, she does not understand what Jesus is saying.

The woman's flippant response leads Jesus to probe more deeply into her marital status (4:16–18). Her moral failings in this arena make her even more uncomfortable, so she shifts the focus of the conversation to the topic of worship sites. Once again, limited by the Bible books they regard as authoritative, Samaritans consider the nearby Mount Gerizim as their holy mountain. This contrasts with the Jews, who regard Mount Zion as the appropriate location for the Lord's temple. Jesus tells the woman that the descendants of Abraham are getting the location right, but he points to a time when the *way* one worships will be more important than *where* that occurs: "Yet a time is coming and has now come when the true worshipers will worship the father in the Spirit and in truth, for they are the kind of worshipers the Father seeks. God is spirit, and his worshipers must worship in the Spirit and in truth" (John 4:23–24).

This conversation has become more than the Samaritan woman bargained for. All she wanted was to draw her water and get home, so she offers an observation that she hopes will shut down any further exchanges. She knows that both Jews and Samaritans are waiting for the dawn of a new era, one in which the Messiah would take the lead in explaining such things more fully. The Hebrew term *Messiah* and its New Testament Greek equivalent, *Christ*, had become the title for the descendant of David who would be set apart by the heavenly Father to redeem the world (2 Samuel 7:11–16; Psalm 2:2; Isaiah 9:6–7). The woman suggests that she and Jesus await his arrival: "I know that Messiah (called Christ) is coming. When he comes, he will explain everything to us" (John 4:25).

What happens next sends a shock wave through the early chapters of John's gospel. No one was getting who Jesus was, so he declares, "I, the one speaking to you—I am he" (John 4:26).

Why would Jesus make such a rare and powerful statement in the middle of Samaria? It is because we have been here before, a fact suggested early in the Samaritan woman's conversation with Jesus. She told him, "our ancestors worshiped on this mountain" (John 4:20). They sure did, and that history made this a place Jesus "had to" go to claim the title of Messiah.

But to make the connection with those Old Testament stories, we need to search using a term other than Sychar. That was the name of the place in the New Testament era, but during Old Testament times, the pass between Mount Ebal and Mount Gerizim hosted a town named Shechem. When we look for Old Testament stories connected to these names, we find that this location hosted some of the most powerful moments of history associated with expectations of the coming Messiah.

The first Shechem story relates to Abram, later known as Abraham. God made three important promises to Abram that shaped the hope of all Old Testament believers: Abram's family would grow to become a great nation, the Lord would give this nation a land of its own, and from that family and on that land, the promised Savior would be born (Genesis 12:1–3). When Abram traveled into the heart of this newly promised land, the Lord appeared to him at Shechem and said, "To your offspring I will give this land" (Genesis 12:7). This is a moment and place that could not be lost to time, so Abram marked the spot with a memorial altar linking the promise to the land.

The next Shechem story involves Abraham's grandson Jacob, returning to the promised land of Canaan after an extended stay in Paddan Aram. Jacob purchased a plot of ground at Shechem and built his own memorial altar (Genesis 33:18–20). Given the theological importance of the place and the memory it carried, Jacob wanted his family to visit this spot often to recall the promises Abraham had received here, so he also dug a well for those who would visit the site (John 4:5–6). This is the very well at which Jesus met the Samaritan woman.

Two more Shechem stories, both involving Joshua, complete the picture. Following the Israelites' four-hundred-year stay in Egypt and forty years in the wilderness, Joshua led the Israelites across the Jordan River—they were taking possession of the land God had promised this nation, land intimately bound to their responsibility of bringing the Messiah into the world. On two occasions, once at the beginning and once at the close of the conquest of Canaan, Joshua brought Israel to Shechem to review their history, their legal obligations to the Almighty, and the important role they played in the salvation plan God had given to Abraham (Joshua 8:30–35; 24:1–28). He built an altar above Shechem on Mount Ebal, inscribing the law code into stone monuments and leading the people to declare their commitment to the plan God had set before them.

Assemble these stories, all of them occurring at one location, and the importance of this place called Shechem or Sychar becomes clear. Before Jerusalem became Israel's religious center, even before Shiloh hosted the Tabernacle, Shechem was the religious focal point of the Old Testament. No geographic location carried greater expectations about the coming Savior from sin, the Messiah. And even though this place was now settled by Samaritans, non-Israelites who had an imperfect understanding of God's plan, it was the perfect place for Jesus to link himself to the title of Messiah. No place had waited longer for his coming. No place had echoed with words of anticipation like the pass between Mount Ebal and Mount Gerizim. That made this a place Jesus "had to" go.

And it is a place *we* need to go as well, because the announcement Jesus makes here can be a source of great comfort. We are people caught up in an eternal problem that we cannot solve on our own: we cannot keep from sinning and the sins we commit destine us to an eternity in hell. God has promised to fix the problem through one person, but who is it? We desperately need to know to whom we can look and in whom we can place our trust.

That is why we have walked with Jesus into Samaria. At Shechem, the Lord confirmed for Abram, Jacob, and all Israel at the time of Joshua that there was only one plan to redeem the world. At Shechem, the Lord repeatedly confirmed that this plan was underway. This is the place people associated with God's plan of salvation and the Messiah's arrival.

When we walk to this location with Jesus, we hear him state in no uncertain terms that *he* is the one the place had been waiting for. And that means he is the one we have been waiting for, the one sent by the Father to rescue us from sin.

This walk with Jesus to Sychar is among the most important we will make. It is a place we also "have to" go. There is only one path to eternal life, opened by just one Savior from sin. We can know that heaven stands open for us because the one on whom the plan depended has come.

14

WALKING WITH JESUS TO MOUNT MOREH

MOST OF OUR WALKS WITH Jesus keep us in sight of Capernaum, his home base. This walk is different. We are on a southward trek into the heart of the Promised Land, a walk that will consume most of the day. After climbing out of the Sea of Galilee basin, we descend steadily from the rolling ridges of Lower Galilee into the sprawling Jezreel Valley. And as the sun dips toward the western horizon, the silhouette of Mount Moreh looms before us.

Just where is Jesus taking us? We are off to Nain, a village on the northern slopes of Mount Moreh. Like Nazareth, five and a half miles to its north, Nain is a small, agricultural village. It is unmentioned in the Old Testament and named in only one verse of the New Testament—Luke 7:11. Without the story we are about to tell, there would be no mention of Nain in the Bible.

Here Jesus performed the first of what would be three stunning miracles of calling the dead back to life. In the future, he will raise the daughter of Jairus in Capernaum (Luke 8:40–56) and his friend Lazarus in Bethany (John 11:1–44). But first, here at Nain, he raises a young man from the dead (Luke 7:11–17). All three miracles demonstrate the great compassion of Jesus, as well as the unequaled power of Jesus over death. But this miracle at Nain is unique in this respect: by it, Jesus securely connected himself to the title *prophet* and all that it means for us.

If you are hoping for a quiet walk, this will not be it. We are pressed on all sides by a noisy crowd. The most recent miracle of Jesus, at Capernaum, caused quite a stir and created quite a following. A centurion had approached Jesus, begging him to heal his servant who was on the verge of dying. Despite the serious nature of his illness and the fact that Jesus never stepped into the presence of the dying man, he was indeed healed (Luke 7:1–10). The news spread like wildfire through Capernaum, and when Jesus left, a large crowd followed him.

As this excited group approaches Nain, a smaller assembly is exiting the village. There is no buzz of excitement surrounding this group—it is a funeral procession, somberly making its way to the cemetery outside the town. In any family, death is a sad and unwelcomed visitor, but the story surrounding this funeral is particularly tragic. The young man who died was the only son of his mother, and she is a widow.

The noisy crowd that accompanies Jesus becomes respectfully silent before this mom who is taking one last walk with her son. There is no hiding her pain, as wave upon wave of grief washes over her. She has walked this road so many times with her son, but no more. Memories flood her mind, and she is unable to contemplate a future without her beloved child.

Others in the funeral procession are thinking about that, because this woman's future is bleak. By law, the family property will transfer to another male in her husband's family. Once her dowry is used up, she will be dependent on the heir of her husband's property. And there is no way of knowing if this heir will be kindly disposed toward her.

Jesus quickly sizes up the situation, and does not wait for anyone to request help. But his first action seems a bit insensitive—instead of quietly stepping aside to allow this funeral procession to pass, Jesus steps right in front of the people carrying the stretcher on which the lifeless body of the young man rests. The procession stops in its tracks.

Now Jesus speaks directly to the deceased. It's almost as if the person had overslept and needed to get on with the day's activities. "Young man, I say to you, get up!" Jesus says (Luke 7:14). Members of both crowds fix their eyes on the corpse, then gasp audibly. In response to Jesus's words, the young man sits up, begins to talk, and jumps off the stretcher to embrace his mother.

So far, the story reveals the deep compassion of Jesus. He senses the pain and disruption in Nain. And he feels compassion for the young man's mother, who was overwhelmed by grief. He then demonstrated his divine power by restoring the life that had been lost.

But there is one more layer of importance to this event, and Luke is not about to let us go until he delivers the grand finale. When they see the miracle, the people of Capernaum and Nain join their voices, praising God and saying, "A great prophet has appeared among us. . . . God has come to help his people" (Luke 7:16). This miracle, performed in this place, results in the recognition of Jesus as a prophet—perhaps even as "the Prophet" (John 1:21; 7:40). This news spreads rapidly throughout Judea and the surrounding countryside.

What does this have to do with Nain? Have we even been here before? At first, it does not seem so. As I noted, Nain is not mentioned in the Old Testament and only this once in the New Testament. But if we pan out a bit and take in the larger geographical context of this New Testament village, we feel the déjà vu.

Nain is on the northern slope of Mount Moreh. On the other side of this mountain, just a mile and a half to the south across a low ridge, is Shunem. We have not visited Nain before in reading the Old Testament, but we have met the neighboring community of Shunem. That is a town with a powerful story, of a prophet who raised a young man from the dead and returned him to his mother.

This Mount Moreh story comes from the time of Elisha (2 Kings 4:8–37). A well-to-do woman had made a room for the prophet, one he could use as he traveled from his home in the Jordan River valley to Samaria. The woman was childless, and her husband quite old. If this situation continued, she would find herself in the same difficult economic circumstances as the widow Jesus met at Nain. Elisha promised this lady that the Lord would honor her kindness to him by providing her with a son. And within the year, that happened.

We now fast-forward to a time when the woman's son had grown old enough to work with this father in the grain fields. There, the boy was gripped by a fierce headache and collapsed. Carried home by a servant, he sat on his mother's lap until he died.

The woman was devastated but rode all the way from Mount Moreh to Mount Carmel, distance of some seventeen miles, to seek help from Elisha. She poured out her grief and frustration at the feet of the prophet, who immediately sent his servant ahead to place Elisha's staff on the face of the young man. But nothing changed. When Elisha arrived, however, he stretched himself out over the young man and life returned to the corpse. The Lord used this event in this place to show his compassion for the grieving and to firmly identify Elisha as his spokesman.

This is the kind of story that sticks to a place. In the future, when parents walked past Shunem on Mount Moreh, they told their children this story. These children told their children, who repeated the story for their children. It is safe to say that by the time Jesus got to Mount Moreh, the story of a prophet raising a young man from the dead was already firmly attached to this mountain.

And Jesus took advantage of that fact. Think of the parallels between this Old Testament story in Shunem and the one that evolves in nearby Nain. In both cases, we see a woman facing difficult emotional and economic circumstances due to the death of her son. In both cases, a man from God restores life and returns the young man to his mother. And both miracles occur on the same mountain, in towns which are just a short walk apart.

Stories far apart in the pages of our Bible reside right next to each other on the land—and in the minds of the people who saw Jesus raise this widow's son. That explains why the people who witnessed Jesus's miracle responded like they did—their language naturally flows from the memories linked to the place: "A great prophet has appeared among us. . . . God has come to help his people" (Luke 7:16).

The people of Nain saw Jesus as the great prophet they were waiting for. This title helps us get to know him a bit better. In the Bible, a prophet was a man or woman who spoke to the people on behalf of the Lord. Sometimes they recounted and interpreted events from the past. Sometimes they gave direction on how to live and think in the present. And at times they foretold future events. But in all cases, they spoke a message on behalf of the Lord.

Prophets like Moses played an important role in Old Testament history. But even he would be eclipsed by a Prophet to come, as the Lord had told Moses: "I will raise up for them a prophet like you from among their fellow Israelites, and I will put my words in his mouth. He will tell them everything I command him" (Deuteronomy 18:18). In the New Testament era, people were waiting for this ultimate Prophet. When they asked John the Baptist, "Are you the Prophet?" (John 1:21), he said no. But when people assigned this title to Jesus, he received it as his own.

He did in Jerusalem, when people referred to him as "the Prophet" (John 7:40), and he did in Nain when he was celebrated as a "great prophet" (Luke 7:16). This is exactly who Jesus was. The other prophets we meet in the Bible were human beings, selected by God to speak to the world on his behalf. But Jesus was more—he was the very Son of God, whom his Father had selected to speak to the world.

And that makes this day-long walk to Nain worth the effort. There are so many voices that compete for our attention. Whose voice can we trust?

A trip to Nain helps answer the question. Think of what this place teaches us about Jesus: He feels deep compassion for us as we navigate the most difficult experiences of life. He has the power to address circumstances that lie well beyond our control. And Jesus is special, not just another in a long line of mortals who speak on behalf of the Almighty. Jesus is the Prophet, the Son of God who has come to earth to speak to us. That is a voice we can trust.

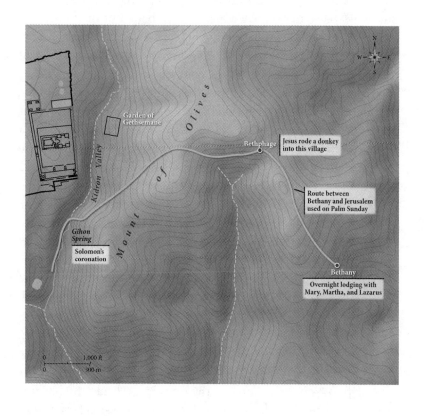

Garden of Gethsemane

Mount of Olives

Kidron Valley

Bethphage

Jesus rode a donkey into this village

Route between Bethany and Jerusalem used on Palm Sunday

Gihon Spring

Solomon's coronation

Bethany

Overnight lodging with Mary, Martha, and Lazarus

N
W   E
S

0   1,000 ft
0   300 m

15

WALKING WITH JESUS
TOWARD THE GIHON SPRING

JESUS ENTERED JERUSALEM MANY TIMES during his life on earth, but only once did he enter to cries of "Hosanna!" Those who shouted their welcome and waved their branches did not realize it at the time, but they were celebrating the first Palm Sunday, the Sunday of Triumphal Entry. The cool morning air echoed with the praise that accompanies our walk down the west side of the Mount of Olives, toward the Kidron Valley.

No worship leader has organized this time of praise. Yet there is a striking similarity in what the people are saying and singing. Everyone is looking for a coronation, the formal crowning of Jesus as their king. And this uniform expectation is not accidental. What Jesus is doing and where he is going recall the coronation of Solomon, and when the crowd notices the symmetry, they call for a king. To be sure, Jesus is a royal descendant of David, but he is not just any king—he is *the King*. That is the title Jesus receives as he moves toward the Gihon Spring.

This walk with Jesus takes place during Passover week. For Jewish families, this week turned their attention to Jerusalem. Among the pilgrims coming to the holy city are Jesus and the disciples. They are not staying within Jerusalem itself, but at the Bethany home of Mary, Martha, and Lazarus. So our morning begins on the east side of the Mount of Olives, a forty-five-minute walk to the holy city.

To reach Jerusalem, we need to walk up the steep eastern slope of the Mount of Olives, cross the mountain's ridge, and then continue down the west side into the Kidron Valley. From here it is a ten-minute walk south to the entry of the city.

That is the plan, at least, but there is a twist, as we have already seen. Just before we get to the top of the ridge, Jesus does something unusual, directing two of the disciples to go ahead to the village of Bethphage to obtain a donkey. They are told to bring it back to him so he can ride into Bethphage and then down the ridge into Jerusalem (Luke 19:28–36). This is a new way for Jesus to enter Jerusalem, marking his final visit and fulfilling the prophecy of Zechariah 9:9: "Rejoice greatly, Daughter Zion! Shout, Daughter Jerusalem! See, your king comes to you, righteous and victorious, lowly and riding on a donkey, on a colt, the foal of a donkey."

Hundreds of ordinary people, unable to afford the inflated price of housing within Jerusalem, have camped out in the olive groves on the west side of the Mount of Olives. When they see Jesus riding a donkey into Jerusalem, they respond the way Zechariah had prophesied they would. They "rejoice greatly" and "shout."

The gospel writers each report a different phrase that circulated through the crowd. Some cry, "Hosanna to the Son of David!" (Matthew 21:9). Others shout, "Blessed is the coming kingdom of our father David!" (Mark 11:10). Still others sing, "Blessed is the king who comes in the name of the Lord!" (Luke 19:38). The language varies from person to person and group to group, but every spirit joins in expectation. They are ready for a new era to begin. They want a coronation. They want to make Jesus their King.

The idea of Messiah as King has deep roots in the Old Testament. The first time we hear such language is at the close of Genesis. In the blessing Jacob gave to Judah, he said, "The scepter will not depart from Judah, nor the ruler's staff from between his feet, until he to whom it belongs shall come and the obedience of the nations shall be his" (Genesis 49:10).

This idea received a significant boost in popularity at the time of King David. The Lord promised him that one of his descendants would rule an eternal kingdom (2 Samuel 7:16). From this point on, biblical authors point to the coming of a *royal* Messiah, an expectation we hear in Zechariah 9:9—"See your king comes to you."

The expectation stirred in the Old Testament carries over into the New Testament. The very first words of Matthew pick up the theme: "This is the genealogy of Jesus the Messiah the son of David" (Matthew 1:1). We hear it in the language of the angel Gabriel, sent to the home of Mary in Nazareth to describe the son she would bear: "He will be great and will be called the Son of the Most High. The Lord God will give him the throne of his father David, and he will reign over Jacob's descendants forever; his kingdom will never end" (Luke 1:32–33).

Anticipation of this King's coming ran particularly high during the festival of Passover. So as the excited crowd sees Jesus as this descendant of David, they commingle language from Psalm 118, which they are accustomed to singing during Passover, with coronation language. "LORD, save us! LORD, grant us success! Blessed is he who comes in the name of the LORD" (Psalm 118:25–26). "Hosanna to the Son of David!" "Blessed is the coming kingdom of our father David!" "Blessed is the king who comes in the name of the Lord!" (Matthew 21:9; Mark 11:10; Luke 19:38).

How does this place contribute to this choice of language? If we lift our eyes from the shouting crowd on the Mount of Olives to the larger geographical context, we sense the déjà vu they are feeling, an impression that affects their words. In this setting, the actions of Jesus look very much like those of Solomon on the day of his coronation (1 Kings 1:28–40).

This is a story of transition, and leadership transitions are always uncertain times. That was particularly true as King David's time was coming to a close. His physical and mental capacities were slipping, yet he had not formally designated a successor. David's ambitious son Adonijah saw this time of uncertainty as an opportunity to advance his own political fortunes, and after securing the support of key advisors from his father's court, he initiated his own coronation ceremony (1 Kings 1:5–10). David knew nothing of it.

As Adonijah's coronation was underway, Bathsheba, Nathan,

and other royal advisors—a group of people not invited to the party—learned of the proceeding and sped into David's presence to inform him. David had promised with an oath that Solomon, Bathsheba's son, would succeed him as king. In his bedroom, David rallied and gave detailed instructions on what should happen next.

The inspired author makes sure we get the details right by presenting them twice—first as David gives the order and again as the order is carried out. Notice the geography: David put Solomon on a mule that had been used exclusively for the king's own royal transportation, and Solomon rode the animal down the ridge of the City of David (opposite the Mount of Olives), to the bottom of the Kidron Valley, stopping at the Gihon Spring. There, Zadok anointed Solomon as king of Israel (1 Kings 1:32–40).

The geography of Solomon's coronation is in full view from the Mount of Olives, and it affects the language of the Palm Sunday crowd welcoming Jesus. Just like Solomon, Jesus is seated on an animal provided by his Father. He is riding to the bottom of the Kidron Valley, toward the Gihon Spring.

The symmetry with Solomon's coronation is unmistakable— history appears to be repeating itself. It looks like a son of David is on his way toward the Gihon Spring, where he will be crowned king of Israel. The place makes the people think "coronation"—so the idea of a *king* is intimately linked to the events of Palm Sunday.

This first use of the title during Passion Week is important to note, because we will hear it used often in coming days to disparage Jesus. The Jewish leaders bring Jesus to Pilate and ask the Roman governor to take action against him, arguing that he is guilty of high treason: Jesus claims to be a king at the expense of Caesar. As Pilate turns to Jesus, we sense mockery as he asks, "Are you the king of the Jews?" (Luke 23:3). Soon, the soldiers who prepare Jesus for crucifixion add their ridicule, dressing him in a scarlet robe and pressing a crown of thorns onto his head. "Then they knelt in front of him and mocked him. 'Hail, king of the Jews!' they said" (Matthew 27:29).

The abuse continues as Jesus hangs on the cross: "If you are the king of the Jews, save yourself" (Luke 23:37). And even when others are silent, the sign posted above his head shouts, "JESUS OF NAZARETH, THE KING OF THE JEWS" (John 19:19). The chief priests, disliking the language, push Pilate to change the message. "Do not write, 'The King of the Jews,' but that this man claimed to be the king of the Jews" (John 19:21). On this matter, Pilate would give them no satisfaction—so the title of *king* hangs over Jesus as he dies on the cross.

In his final hours, Jesus was repeatedly linked to the title of *king* in contemptuous fashion. If we let that influence our perception of Jesus as King, we will miss the great comfort the title offers.

Palm Sunday certifies that Jesus *is* our King. He is poised to do for us what mortal kings did for their subjects. So let's consider what was expected of a king in Bible times.

The king provided his subjects with structure—he was the one who made sure the lives of ordinary people had a predictable and satisfying rhythm. The king provided protection from anyone intending to harm his subjects, leading his own army in battle against invading nations. The king was responsible for establishing and maintaining a just society, one in which the socially and economically powerful did not take advantage of the powerless.

No matter what type of political system we live under now, we crave a King who truly looks out for us. We will have that in Jesus. But for now, when life becomes so challenging that we cry out for help, we can use the words of Psalm 118, the song the worshipers sang on Palm Sunday. "When hard pressed, I cried to the LORD; he brought me into a spacious place. The LORD is with me; I will not be afraid. What can mere mortals do to me? The LORD is with me; he is my helper. I look in triumph on my enemies. . . . LORD, save us! LORD, grant us success! Blessed is he who comes in the name of the LORD" (vv. 5–7, 25–26).

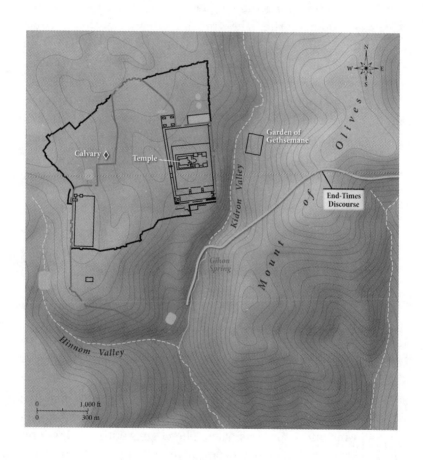

Calvary ◇

Temple

Garden of
Gethsemane

O l i v e s

Kidron Valley

End-Times
Discourse

Gihon
Spring

M o u n t   o f

Hinnom Valley

N
W   E
S

0	1,000 ft
0	300 m

16

WALKING WITH JESUS ABOVE
THE KIDRON VALLEY

WHAT IS THE NEXT BIG thing? It could be an acceptance letter from a college or a job offer after graduation. It could be a wedding, the birth of a child or grandchild, or a long-anticipated vacation. Life is full of change, so we are prone to ask, what is the next big thing?

As we walk with Jesus above the Kidron Valley, up the steep slope of the Mount of Olives, he talks about the next big thing on the divine calendar—his return to earth as Judge. This declaration comes at the end of a long discourse Jesus gives in response to a question of the disciples: "What will be the sign of your coming and of the end of the age?" (Matthew 24:3).

Jesus provides a thumbnail sketch of what the disciples can expect before the end. But on that last day, the culminating moment will be when Jesus sits on his throne and judges the world. In this chapter, we will explore the connection between the title *judge* and the Kidron Valley. And we will see how this important title of Jesus plays a role in our own lives.

This walk with Jesus begins at the Temple complex in Jerusalem. The disciples are awestruck by the grand buildings, and understandably so (Matthew 24:1). These men are rural folks, most familiar with the simple architecture found in their home villages. There, buildings are small and utilitarian in design, standing in sharp contrast to the enormous and uniquely adorned buildings on the Temple Mount. The disciples assume that buildings like these in the Temple complex will never go away.

Jesus is less impressed. "Do you see all these things?" he asks.

"Truly I tell you, not one stone here will be left on another; every one will be thrown down" (Matthew 24:2). As impressive as these buildings are, they will be ruins in less than forty years. Jesus is speaking about the destruction of the Temple complex by the Romans that will occur in AD 70. In doing so, he delivers a jolt of reality that will drive the disciples' vision forward to the next big thing.

That is the kind of statement that stops people in their tracks. We notice things getting quiet for a while as the disciples walk up the western slope of the Mount of Olives on their way back to Bethany. Along the way, Jesus stops, sits down, and gazes back into the Kidron Valley. It is time to break the silence and start a conversation, and it is the view into the Kidron Valley that influences the topic.

The disciples had asked to know what was next. "'Tell us,' they said, 'when will this happen, and what will be the sign of your coming and of the end of the age?'" (Matthew 24:3). Perhaps they assume that an event as devastating as the destruction of the Temple would immediately usher in the end times, so Jesus begins his answer by listing the things that would take place before the final day. The destruction of the Temple would not be the worst of it.

In days to come, there would be religious deception, international unrest, natural disasters, persecution of believers, and loveless behavior in the extreme (Matthew 24:4–12). Despite all those challenges, "this gospel of the kingdom will be preached in the whole world" (Matthew 24:14). Then and only then will the final day arrive, heralded by unusual behavior in the celestial bodies and a loud trumpet call signaling the angels to gather the entire world to one place for judgment (Matthew 24:29–31).

But the disciples want more information, like a precise date for these culminating events. Jesus does not offer that. Instead, he uses allusions and parables that revolve around this theme: "Therefore keep watch, because you do not know the day or the hour" (Matthew 25:13)

The next big thing is this same Jesus, the one who sits with the disciples on this mountain, taking a seat in this geographic arena again. The next time, he will be on a throne. "When the Son of Man comes in his glory, and all the angels with him, he will sit on his glorious throne," Jesus says. "All the nations will be gathered before him, and he will separate the people one from another as a shepherd separates the sheep from the goats. He will put the sheep on his right and the goats on his left" (Matthew 25:31–33). Those on the right will enjoy an eternal inheritance, living in peace and joy, while those on the left will go away to a place of eternal punishment. This is Jesus functioning as Judge.

It's the first time we get a more detailed picture of Jesus in this role. On earlier walks, we heard him speak about a coming day when the population of the world would be divided into two groups. In the parable of the weeds, Jesus talked about leaving the wheat (believers) and weeds (unbelievers) in the field until the harvest, when the wheat and weeds would face very different ends (Matthew 13:24–30). The events of the last day were also pictured by a net that gathers good and bad fish indiscriminately from the lake; at the close of the fishing trip, they would be separated (Matthew 13:47–50).

But who will be the one making these decisions about where people spend eternity? Jesus has dropped hints before (see John 5:22; 8:26), but he's never said it as clearly as he does here. *He* is the one who will judge the world on the last day.

What does this declaration have to do with the Kidron Valley? As he did so often, Jesus waited to teach a lesson until he was in just the right place. He speaks of his role as Judge above the Kidron Valley, in the place that Old Testament believers associated with divine judgment and the end times.

On several occasions, reforming kings destroyed pagan idols and worship tools in the Kidron Valley. It was here that King Asa did what was right in God's eyes by expelling shrine prostitutes from the land, getting rid of idols, and burning the image associated with the worship of Asherah (1 Kings 15:12–13). King Hezekiah reversed the policies of his wicked father, Ahaz, cleansing the Temple by removing all the pagan objects inside and destroying them in the Kidron Valley (2 Chronicles 29:16; 30:14). And King Josiah also did what was right, clearing out the pagan items, destroying them, and depositing their remains in the Kidron Valley. This is mentioned no less than three times (2 Kings 23:4, 6, 12). Taken together, these facts show why people thought of divine judgment when they looked into the Kidron Valley.

But there is more. The prophet Joel spoke not of some general divine judgment but of a particular, final day of judgment associated with the Kidron Valley. In Joel's day, more than 850 years before Jesus spoke of himself as Judge, the people of Israel were facing an agricultural catastrophe. A locust invasion was devastating the farm fields and threatening the nation's food supply. Joel saw this as a divine judgment and called for the people to repent: "Rend your heart and not your garments. Return to the LORD your God, for he is gracious and compassionate, slow to anger and abounding in love, and he relents from sending calamity" (Joel 2:13). The prophet spoke this way because the terrible locust plague was not the worst of it.

Joel saw a day coming when the Lord would gather all people of all time for judgment. This day of judgment, a day of rewards and retribution, would take place in a valley near Jerusalem, one that Joel called the Valley of Jehoshaphat (Joel 3:2, 12). *Jehoshaphat* is a Hebrew expression meaning "the Lord judges."

The third chapter of Joel is the only place in the Bible that the label "the Valley of Jehoshaphat" appears. Where exactly is it? We have already seen a connection between the Kidron Valley and divine judgment. And the prophet Zechariah associated judgment at the final day with the Mount of Olives (Zechariah 14:1–4). It seems that the identification of this "Valley of Jehoshaphat" by the early church was correct—the place that Joel said would host the final judgment is the Kidron Valley.

That is why Jesus uses this setting to speak in greater detail about his role as Judge. This is a master teacher at work—place and topic come together to make everything Jesus says clearer and more memorable. He has not spoken in detail about his role as Judge before; he waited until this moment to give the last long lecture of his public ministry, a discourse on the last things, spoken during the final week of his ministry on earth, in a place that the Old Testament linked to the last day.

So how are we to feel about this walk with Jesus?

Most of us would be uncomfortable going to court. Even if we are innocent, there is a shadow of uncertainty that comes with standing before a judge. So how would we feel about standing before the Judge who is about to announce our eternal destiny?

The facts of our case are clear: we are guilty as charged. Our Creator has called for each of us to live sin-free life, but we have lived lives that are sin-filled. That makes the Mount of Olives and Kidron Valley, long associated with divine judgment, an uncomfortable and threatening place—that is, unless we notice with whom we are walking.

To be sure, Jesus is the Judge who will determine where we spend our eternity. To be sure, we are guilty as charged. But this Jesus, the one who is my Judge, is also my defense attorney. Even more than that, he is the Savior who suffered and died in my place, absorbing the punishment for my sin.

And while the heavenly Father promised to punish sin, he never said he would do that twice. Jesus knows this better than anyone. The punishment is taken. What's done is done. So I know the Judge's verdict even before I stand in front of him. "Come, you who are blessed by my Father; take your inheritance, the kingdom prepared for you since the creation of the world" (Matthew 25:34). That is the next big thing.

As Jesus walked from place to place, he met new people who needed to know who he was, what skills he had, and how he viewed the experiences of human beings. Jesus used his professional titles to provide that introduction.

In this section, we have walked with Jesus to places associated with Old Testament professional titles. And we have seen that Jesus selected these places to more fully reveal himself as the one who completely lived out those titles. That makes them places of growth for us—we learn who Jesus was and what roles he is anxious to play in our lives.

These walks have taken us all over the map of Israel. Near the Samaritan village of Sychar, Jesus identified himself as the Messiah. At Mount Moreh, he was recognized as the Prophet. On the Mount of Olives, we met him as King. And sitting on that same mountain above the Kidron Valley, Jesus presented himself as the Judge of the world. Jesus has invited us to walk to these places with him because they help us better understand both the titles and each of his roles in our lives.

1. What does your professional title or job description tell others about you? When have you seen a relationship between job titles and places?

2. How was the Old Testament title *Messiah* linked to Sychar? What does it mean for you that Jesus is the Messiah?

3. How was the Old Testament title *Prophet* linked to Mount Moreh? What does it mean for you that Jesus is the Prophet?

4. How was the Old Testament title *King* linked to the Gihon Spring? What does it mean for you that Jesus is the King?

5. How was the Old Testament title *Judge* linked to the Kidron Valley? What does it mean for you that Jesus is the Judge?

6. As you navigate your current season of life, which of these titles is most helpful to you?

PART FIVE

Jesus, Geography, and Our Mission

"I WISH THAT I COULD stay longer but I have to . . ." No matter how you complete that sentence, it will end with a reference to one of your many missions in life. I don't have to tell you that that there are often more things to do than time in which to do them. That means we need to prioritize. But, as we do, we need to realize that one mission is more important than any of the others—the mission Jesus gave us, the sequel to the mission he accomplished.

Jesus talks about this mission with some frequency. And at this point in our study, it will come as no surprise that Jesus teaches about our mission in the world by taking us to specific places.

We have been to these places before, but this time the geographic déjà vu is different. The stories we discussed earlier took us to places we had seen before as readers of the Old Testament. In this part of our study, we will not have to turn as many pages, because we will revisit places we have been before with Jesus. He invites us to see how the story and the lesson grow the second time around.

Each of the four places we walk in this part of the book speaks to our mission of introducing the Kingdom to others. We will walk with Jesus to the Decapolis to see how powerful the telling of our story can be. We will walk to Bethany and hear what Jesus says to us about developing our faith so it can produce a convincing witness. We will walk with Jesus to Mount Hermon for a lesson on Satan's effort to undo our mission. And, finally, we will walk to Mount Arbel for a lesson on the scope of our mission as followers of Christ.

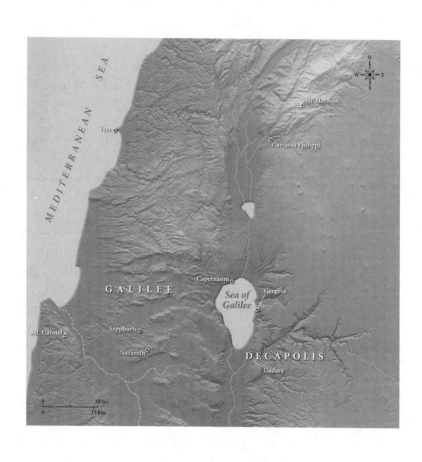

17

WALKING WITH JESUS
TO THE DECAPOLIS

OUR FIRST WALK WITH JESUS takes us to the Decapolis. This region is very different from the one in which we typically spend time with him. Most of our walks occur on the western side of the Sea of Galilee, in the region of Galilee. Now, we are going to the eastern side of the lake, "the other side" both in terms of geography and culture. Jesus will take us to this area, called the Decapolis, on two different occasions, showing us the substantial change that occurs when a new convert tells his story of meeting the Lord.

The first Decapolis story introduces us to a man in deep trouble (Mark 5:1–20). As soon as we cross the Sea of Galilee on a boat, before we can take many steps on the eastern shore, we meet him. He is alone, shunned by the people who know him. His incredible strength and penchant for violence provokes the sort of fear that guarantees his isolation from others. The man lives in the cemetery, among those who neither protest his presence nor offer him companionship. Sadly, his violent disposition is often turned inward, as he cuts himself with stones. This poor man lives a miserable life, because he has been infiltrated by dozens of demons.

Jesus treats the man differently than others do. Jesus doesn't run away when this man runs screaming toward him. Nor does Jesus hold the man up as an object lesson, a picture of what happens when you make company with fallen angels. No, when the man approaches, our Savior is filled with compassion and sets about freeing him from his demons.

This man's legs carry him toward Jesus, but it is the demons who speak. Knowing they are outmatched, they bargain for a less permanent fate than the one they know is coming. Jesus doesn't bargain, but he does send the demons from the man into a nearby herd of pigs. Doing what demons do, they immediately harm their new hosts. The possessed pigs rush down the steep ridge on which they are feeding, drowning themselves in the Sea of Galilee.

Mark concludes his account by inviting us to see how those impacted by the miracle respond. The people herding the pigs are suddenly without a job, so they go into town to report on the miracle and the economic loss the community has just experienced. The people who hear their story came out to see for themselves what has happened.

Amazingly, the townsfolk are more fearful of Jesus, whom they do not know, than of the demons they had known, and they plead with Jesus to leave the region. And what of the man Jesus has released from demon possession? When he sees Jesus heading for the boat, he pleads to go along, desperate to remain near the one who had changed his life. But that is not God's plan. "Jesus did not let him, but said, 'Go home to your own people and tell them how much the Lord has done for you, and how he has had mercy on you.' So the man went away and began to tell in the Decapolis how much Jesus had done for him. And all the people were amazed" (Mark 5:19–20).

We don't turn many pages in our Bible before we walk back into this region with Jesus (Mark 7:31–8:13). But now we hardly recognize the place.

The large herd of pigs that once fed on the hillside is gone, replaced by thousands of people who have come to be with Jesus. They bring the sick and disabled for healing. And as their desire to learn from Jesus stretches into a third day, their food gives out. The disciples go searching but locate only seven loaves of bread and a few small fish, barely enough to put a dent in the problem. That is until Jesus blesses this small amount of food and miraculously multiplies it to feed four thousand households. The people are sated, and the disciples collect seven baskets of leftovers.

Both stories occur in the same region, which makes the change we see even more stunning. These are both Decapolis stories, occurring on the other side of the Sea of Galilee (Matthew 8:28; Mark 5:1), "across the lake from Galilee" (Luke 8:26). This puts us on the east side of the water. Mark calls it the "region of the Gerasenes," a label that has challenged biblical geographers. I think the best solution is to take this as a reference to the area around a town that later became known as Kursi.

This interpretation is supported by a fifth-century Christian religious compound built here to recall the miracle, as well as the topography that lies just to the south of Kursi. In the story, the pigs ran down a ridge into the lake; the only place on the east side of the Sea of Galilee where the topography would allow that is just south of this religious complex at Kursi.

In the end, any question about the location is resolved when Mark uses the better-known name for the region: the Decapolis (Mark 5:20). The story of the feeding of the four thousand also lives at the same address, as Mark locates Jesus in the Decapolis area (Mark 7:31).

In these two stories, we need to be certain of where we are—because the location highlights the dramatic change that occurs in the people here. Consider the details Mark includes, factors that an observant Jewish person living on the west side of the lake would see as indicating the non-Jewish character of the place. In the Jewish culture, tombs were unclean, but here we find a man living in a cemetery, a point Mark mentions three times (5:2, 3, 5). In the Jewish culture, pigs are not kosher (Leviticus 11:7; Deuteronomy 14:8), yet here we find thousands of pigs being raised. In the Jewish culture, nakedness is shameful (Genesis 9:22–23), but here we find a man running around without clothing (Luke 8:27). It was the kind of place the demons saw as their own, and they begged Jesus not to send them "out of the area" (Mark 5:10). Not everyone living in the Decapolis was demon possessed, of course, but the description of this one man confirms the basic premise of observant Jews living in the first century: the Decapolis was a godless place to be shunned.

Ethnically, this was a Gentile world. When local people spoke of God, they used language that revealed their distance, calling him the "God of Israel" (Matthew 15:31). This fact is also highlighted even by the number of baskets of leftovers collected at the close of the feeding miracle. Unlike the feeding of the five thousand, after which the disciples collected twelve baskets (a number associated with the twelve tribes of Israel), the seven baskets here are a cultural marker that points to Gentiles (Deuteronomy 7:1; Matthew 16:8–12). Put all these details together and you see Jesus in an area where people are steeped in the superstitions of a pagan worldview. If people are going to change here, it will be over the objection of many cultural obstacles.

It is the very unlikeliness of change that makes the change we see between these two stories so dramatic. The demon-possessed man was not Jewish, met Jesus only once, and had no experience as an evangelist. He talked to people who had no background in the Old Testament and no expectation of a coming Messiah. The religion they knew had hundreds of gods, not one. And their first experience with Jesus left them so terrified that they asked him to leave (Mark 5:15, 17).

What a different story during our second walk into the region! The people who had asked Jesus to leave came out by the thousands to welcome him. They brought their sick and disabled friends and family members, seeking healing. They praised Jesus. And they stayed and stayed even when hunger pangs urged them to leave. What accounts for the difference? The fact that one man told them how much the Lord had done for him.

That is one reason Jesus brings us back to the Decapolis. Our mission entails telling our story about Jesus, and here he wants to show us what can happen when we do just that. Truth be told, we often set our expectations too low. We may be new to the Christian faith and feel that we need more experience with Jesus before we can tell our story. We may have concerns that the questions people might ask will exceed our understanding. We may believe our story lacks interest or power, or that we should wait and tell our story to an audience less distant from the Lord. Each of those excuses, however, is defeated by reading these two Decapolis stories together.

The Holy Spirit can use our own stories to draw others to Jesus, no matter what we think of ourselves or to whom we are speaking. The question is not whether we have a story to share, but whether or not we *will*. Jesus speaks these words to us as well: "Go home to your own people and tell them how much the Lord has done for you, and how he has had mercy on you" (Mark 5:19).

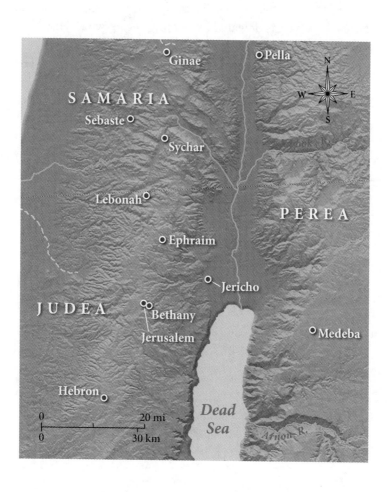

18

WALKING WITH JESUS TO BETHANY

THE BEST-KNOWN BETHANY STORY IS the one in which Jesus raised Lazarus from the dead. This is an important story, deserving all the attention it gets, demonstrating the power of Jesus over death. But this story, likes its geographical partner, also shines a spotlight on Lazarus's sisters, Mary and Martha. In Luke 10:38–42, four of the five verses consist of a dialogue between Martha and Jesus. In John 11:17–44, Jesus and Martha interact in a third of the verses.

In the first Bethany story, the Holy Spirit highlights the choice Martha made about how to listen to Jesus. In the second Bethany account, the Holy Spirit highlights the consequences of Martha's choice when she faced the death of her brother. Because our Christian mission is built on the strength of our faith witness—and because our faith witness is particularly powerful at times of personal challenge—the growth of our faith is fundamental to our successful Christian service. In our second trip to Bethany, we will see that a faith prepared to meet the great challenges of life develops not just from listening to Jesus but listening to Jesus with undivided attention.

We find the more familiar story in John 11, in a passage that concludes with Jesus raising Lazarus from the dead. This story takes place in a small, rural village a little less than two miles east of Jerusalem. This proximity to Jerusalem made Bethany a valuable place for Jesus to spend the night, and it was here that he developed a warm friendship with these three siblings.

We do not know the location of their house, but we presume it would have been within the ancient village that lies beneath the modern village of el-ʿAzariyeh. Its Arabic name is related to our

English word *Lazarus*. The ancient village was very different from
Jerusalem, having no large public buildings and no busy public
market. It was a quiet place, but close enough to Jerusalem that
Jesus could stay there and walk to Jerusalem in about forty minutes.

John 11 opens with disturbing news: Lazarus, who has been
gravely ill, has died. His sudden and unexpected death shakes
the world of his surviving sisters, Mary and Martha, who feel the
overwhelming grief any of us would at the death of a family member. Their energy sapped, the sisters grieve at home; it is Jewish
tradition for them to remain here for seven days, receiving friends
and family. At the start of the story, the women are gaining comfort
from people they know and love.

But some of the visitors are becoming reckless and unhelpful
with their words. They know that the miracle-working Jesus had
a close relationship with this family, and they begin to voice an
only-slightly-veiled criticism: "Could not he who opened the eyes
of the blind man have kept this man from dying?" (John 11:37).
Both sisters are stung by the question (11:21, 32).

One other detail sharpens our understanding of the sisters'
mood. It is now the fourth day since Lazarus had died (11:17, 39).
Within their Jewish culture, most people believe that the soul of
someone who has died remains near the body for three days—
within this time, it is possible for life to return. But by the start
of the fourth day, people believe that the soul is locked out of the
body. Mary and Martha are standing toe-to-toe with this disturbing viewpoint when word reaches them that Jesus is on the way.

At this point in the story, Martha moves to the foreground.
She doesn't wait for Jesus to arrive or for him to call for her as
Mary would (compare John 11:20 and 28–29). Instead, Martha
goes out to confront Jesus. "Lord," she says, "if you had been here,
my brother would not have died. But I know that even now God
will give you whatever you ask" (John 11:21). There is a presumption in Martha's words and actions, an edge that is only slightly
softened by the vague hope that something good may yet come

of this situation. But we are ready to give her the benefit of the doubt—after all, her brother has just died.

Jesus trades the vague hope of Martha's language for the certainty of a future reunion. "Your brother will rise again," he says (John 11:23). But Martha's thoughts go to the far horizon of this world's history. She replies, "I know he will rise again in the resurrection at the last day" (John 11:24).

Jesus counters with the idea of a more imminent reunion. "I am the resurrection and the life. The one who believes in me will live, even though they die; and whoever lives by believing in me will never die. Do you believe this?" (John 11:25–26). Here the spotlight moves to Martha's faith: Does she believe that reunion is possible today? Does she believe that Jesus can raise the dead? "Yes, Lord," she replies, "I believe that you are the Messiah, the Son of God, who is to come into the world" (John 11:27).

But as the story goes on, we sense a conflict between what Martha knows and what she believes. She knows there will be a second coming and a great resurrection of the dead. She knows Jesus is the Messiah, capable of raising the dead. But the deepest form of faith involves more than knowing—it means that you *trust* what you know. Martha is not yet there.

This becomes evident as we move to the tomb of Lazarus, just outside the village of Bethany. Jesus calls for the removal of the stone blocking the entrance of the tomb. Martha stands at his side, about to witness one of the great miracles of all time, about to be reunited with her beloved brother. And this is where the void between her knowing and believing becomes obvious.

Martha objects to the opening of the tomb. Nothing good can come of it. "But Lord," she says, "by this time there is a bad odor, for he has been there four days." Jesus replies to her, "Did I not tell you that if you believe, you will see the glory of God?" (John 11:39–40). She knows, but struggles to believe.

At this moment, the geographical déjà vu kicks in again. We remember that we have been in Bethany before, in the home of

Mary, Martha, and Lazarus. And when we read that story carefully in Luke 10:38–42, we see that it reveals the root of Martha's problem.

This is a much shorter Bethany story. It begins by stating that the siblings had opened their home to Jesus and the collection of disciples traveling with him (Luke 10:38). Then, as today, when you opened your house to someone, you took on several responsibilities. In the first century, the host family supplied the guests not only with shelter but with food—and serving a meal to Jesus and his entourage required prep time. With all those responsibilities looming over the women, Jesus began to teach within the home. Now Mary and Martha had to make a choice. How could they balance this opportunity to listen to Jesus with the responsibility of providing hospitality?

The story centers on the fact that Mary and Martha make different choices. Martha tries to do it all. The house is small, and Jesus's voice carries through it easily. So Martha chooses to listen while she works. Luke describes her as "distracted by all the preparations that had to be made" (10:40). Jesus says that she is "worried and upset about many things" (10:41). Martha's attempt at multitasking has consequences. She cannot listen as effectively or reflect on what Jesus is teaching.

Mary, though, makes a different choice. She assumes the posture of a student by sitting at Jesus's feet—an opportunity typically not offered by a male Jewish teacher. Mary sets aside the pressing array of responsibilities of the host family, choosing to listen attentively with a full focus on Jesus.

Mary's choice angers Martha, and she lets everyone know it. Martha stops her food preparation and takes up a position next to Jesus. We notice her glaring at her sister, who is sitting on the ground next to Jesus, as she says, "Lord, don't you care that my sister has left me to do the work by myself? Tell her to help me!" (Luke 10:40).

Jesus seizes upon this teachable moment. Everyone in the house could see that there was a difference in how these two sisters were listening, and Jesus makes it clear that one of the choices is better than the other. "Martha, Martha," he says to her, "you are worried and upset about many things but few things are needed—or indeed only one. Mary has chosen what is better, and it will not be taken away from her" (Luke 10:41–42).

Mary had given her full attention to Jesus. As she pondered his words in her mind, the Holy Spirit anchored them in her heart. But Martha's way of listening, compromised by her distraction and worry, did not bring her to the same place. She knew what Jesus was saying, but she had not created space in her life for the Spirit to anchor it to her very core. Mary had chosen the better course, and it made a difference when life became hard.

That has not changed. Jesus still calls for us to listen to him. And how we listen affects who we become. I confess that I often listen to Jesus in the way Martha did—every day is filled with so many things to do, and I want to think that by multitasking, by doing more than one thing at the same time, I am getting more done. But this is a myth. My "multitasking" is really sequential tasking—not doing two things at the same time but a rapid shifting of my focus from one thing to another. It limits the quality of my work on either task, and both suffer for it.

That is the Martha in me. But I don't want to listen to Jesus in that way, to be distracted and worried about other things. Jesus's words to Martha call me to give him my time and attention, so that he does not have to compete with other things in my life. "Few things are needed," Jesus said, "or indeed only one. Mary has chosen what is better, and it will not be taken away from her" (Luke 10:42).

To accomplish my mission, I need a strong faith, a faith that gives a powerful witness on even the most difficult days. This pair of Bethany stories teaches both how that faith grows and why it is important to my mission. This is the lesson we have walked to Bethany to learn: faith that prepares us to meet the great challenges of life grows not just from listening to Jesus but listening with undivided attention.

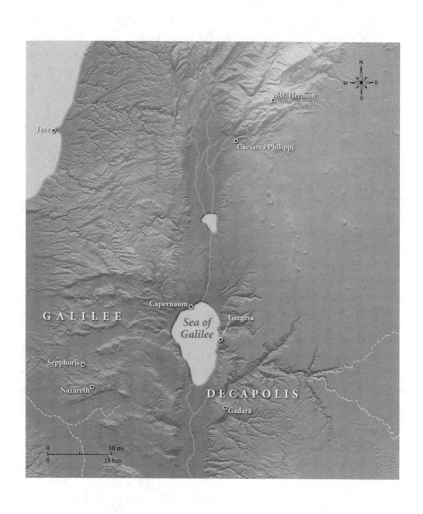

19

WALKING WITH JESUS TO MOUNT HERMON

COLLEGE AND PROFESSIONAL SPORTS TEAMS prepare for games by researching their opponents. "Scouts" spend hours watching game film, looking for their opponents' patterns of play and weaknesses that could be exploited. No matter what the sport, having this knowledge makes it more likely you will succeed.

The same principle applies in our battle with Satan. He does all he can to disrupt the growth and stability of God's Kingdom on earth, so it would be helpful for us to have a "scouting report" on him. And we get something like that as we walk with Jesus to Mount Hermon. In this location, Satan confronts Jesus twice. We can use what we learn in these attacks to better combat the devil's attacks on us and on our churches.

The first Mount Hermon story we will consider finds us in "the region of Caesarea Philippi" (Matthew 16:13). Jesus takes the disciples on a field trip to the southern base of Mount Hermon, outside their usual work area around the Sea of Galilee. He chooses this location for a reason. As we saw in chapter 10, the southern ridge of Mount Hermon is a pagan shrine. With that sanctuary to false gods as a backdrop, Jesus asks the disciples to reflect on who he is and what he can do. How does he size up against the claims of power and authority made by the deities represented at the base of this mountain?

Peter sets Jesus apart from all of them, saying, "You are the Messiah, the Son of the living God" (Matthew 16:16). Jesus celebrates this confession by responding, "I tell you that you are Peter, and on this rock I will build my church" (Matthew 16:18).

Jesus wants the disciples to fully understand who he is because this location marks a turning point in his life. "From that time on

Jesus began to explain to his disciples that he must go to Jerusalem and suffer many things at the hands of the elders, the chief priests and the teachers of the law, and that he must be killed and on the third day be raised to life" (Matthew 16:21). This final trip to Jerusalem is not optional. And, lest the disciples miss the point, Jesus will repeat the nature and necessity of his journey two more times in coming days (17:22–23; 20:17–19). The story has to progress to Jerusalem, for that is where the Son of Man will "give his life as a ransom for many" (Matthew 20:28).

To say the least, all the disciples are stunned by the thought. But only Peter is impulsive enough to stand strongly against it. He does not ask for clarification, and he does not politely ask if Jesus would be willing to reconsider. True to form, Peter attacks the idea aggressively, taking Jesus aside to rebuke him. "Never, Lord!" he says. "This shall never happen to you!" (Matthew 16:22). Although a suffering Messiah was clearly taught in Old Testament passages like Isaiah 53, Peter is not about to let *his* Messiah go down that road.

The voice is Peter's, but the speech is that of Satan. And Jesus is not about to let the devil hide himself behind Peter. Jesus says to Peter, "Get behind me, Satan! You are a stumbling block to me; you do not have in mind the concerns of God, but merely human concerns" (Matthew 16:23). Back when Peter had given his powerful confession of Jesus as Messiah, the voice was his own but the thoughts were God's (Matthew 16:17). This second time Peter speaks, the source is far less noble. He is speaking for Satan.

But just who is Satan? He is a created spirit who turned from the cause of God to the cause of evil. Although condemned to an eternity of hell fire, he has been allowed by God to prowl the earth like a roaring lion, "looking for someone to devour" (1 Peter 5:8). Satan gobbles up people just like he did Adam and Eve, using the lies that are his native language (John 8:44)—he presents sin as a virtue and virtue as vice, and he characterizes the Creator as an uncaring dictator while presenting himself as a loving friend. At the base of Mount Hermon, we see Satan at work, using the voice of Jesus's dear friend to try to keep the Lord away from Jerusa-lem—away from the cross.

And there is the déjà vu. We have heard this voice on an earlier walk to Mount Hermon.

For the full story, we need to turn back in our Bibles, from Mat-thew 16 to Matthew 4. John had just baptized Jesus in the Jordan River. The Father in heaven used this moment to make crystal clear that Jesus is his special Son, the one he sent to redeem the world from sin.

Satan had known he was in for a fight with a unique descendant of Eve (Genesis 3:15). But who would it be? Taking no chances, he had successfully attacked and destroyed the spiritual health of every descendant of Eve. Even the great ones had fallen, from Abraham and Sarah to Moses and David. But now the Father had revealed his Son, and Satan would direct his temptation at this particular descendant of Eve. At the start of his fourth chapter, Matthew describes three temptations that Satan turned loose on Jesus, the third of which occurs on Mount Hermon.

We know this temptation happened here, even though Matthew makes the geographical connection a little harder to see. He is not in the habit of providing proper names for mountains, only descrip-tions—so in the case of the third temptation, Matthew says the devil took Jesus to "a very high mountain and showed him all the kingdoms of the world and their splendor" (4:8). There are many mountains in the Promised Land, but only one fits that description.

To illustrate how Mount Hermon stands out, consider this: Mount Meron, the second-highest mountain in the region, rises 3,963 feet in elevation. But that is a distant second to Mount Her-mon, soaring to an elevation of 9,232 feet. Just as important is the fact that Mount Hermon is not a single peak but a sprawling ridge covering more than 350 square miles and dominating the horizon. The "very high mountain" of Matthew must be unique from other mountains in this land. Given its elevation and size, there is no better candidate than Mount Hermon.

We can further support this identification by considering how Satan used the "very high mountain" to show Jesus the kingdoms and splendor of the world. Of course, no mountain in the world is high enough to give of a view of every nation. But in Bible times you could see representatives of the entire world and their trade goods by standing on the south side of Mount Hermon. This mountain is so dominating, so high in elevation, that merchants moving trade goods had no choice but to avoid its steep slopes and snow-covered summit. They moved along its eastern flanks.

Another obstacle, the Huleh Basin, shaped where people went south of Mount Hermon. This thirty-thousand-acre basin was a swamp in Bible times, and travelers avoided it by using a relatively narrow piece of dry ground that lay just south of Caesarea Philippi. Here, where ancient travel options were limited by mountain and swamp, you could see "the kingdoms of the world and their splendor," making Mount Hermon the most likely place for Jesus to wrestle with the third temptation of Satan.

This temptation took advantage of the location. Satan offered Jesus the right to rule all those kingdoms he could see represented below him, without having to go to the cross. "All this I will give you," Satan said, "if you will bow down and worship me" (Matthew 4:9).

Let's start our analysis by realizing that this offer was built on a false premise. The kingdoms of the world did not belong to Satan—yet he slyly and smoothly made the pitch to Jesus as if the world were his to offer. What did he want in return? All Jesus needed to do was fall to the ground and acknowledge that Satan was supreme, by worshiping him.

Interestingly, Matthew used the same language just two chapters earlier to describe what the wise men did when they saw young Jesus: "they bowed down and worshiped him" (2:11). Satan's request was an assault on the very first commandment, and Jesus was not taken in. He responded with the clear words of his Father, as recorded in Deuteronomy 6:13. Jesus said, "Away from me,

Satan! For it is written: 'Worship the Lord your God, and serve him only'" (Matthew 4:10).

The similarities between the two Mount Hermon stories are striking. First, we note that they occur in the same location—if we are organizing our Bibles geographically, we will quickly link the stories and see what they teach about how Satan works and how we can defeat him. Second, we see that Satan came to tempt Jesus at critical times during his ministry on earth—in Matthew 4, Jesus had just begun his public ministry; in Matthew 16, Jesus made the final turn toward Jerusalem to complete his mission on the cross. Failure at either of these moments would have a far-reaching impact on his mission. Third, in both cases Satan presented himself as someone who was trying to help—Jesus wanted a universal kingdom, Satan would give it to him; Jesus was on the way to Jerusalem to suffer and die, Satan used Peter to discourage the trip. Finally, the Greek phrase Jesus used to confront and dismiss Satan is the same in both stories, though it is often translated in different ways in English translations—"Get away from me, Satan!" No negotiation. No arguing. No name calling. Just a simple, *Get away!*

Our mission as followers of Christ will bring us into conflict with the Lord's sworn enemy. By walking with Jesus to Mount Hermon and examining his experiences there with Satan, we get a better idea of what to expect and how to respond. We can anticipate Satan's attack at critical moments, so we should be on guard at turning points in our spiritual life—or the life of our church.

At such moments, we need to identify Satan by the nature of the message rather than voice he uses, since he can speak even through trusted friends and church leaders. We will know that Satan is speaking when we recognize lies—he will offer a course of action that has a certain appeal, at least until we realize it violates God's will.

The more we know about Satan's patterns of play, the more easily we will recognize the temptation he brings. Then we can respond as Jesus did: "Get away!"

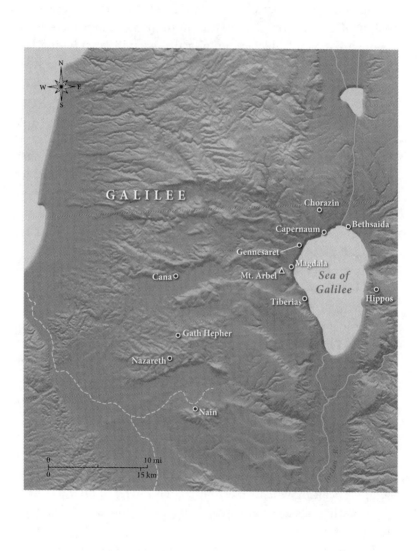

20

WALKING WITH JESUS TO MOUNT ARBEL

OUR FINAL WALK WITH JESUS connects us to the final words he spoke in Galilee.

After Jesus died on the cross and rose from the dead, he instructed the disciples to leave Jerusalem and meet him in Galilee (Matthew 28:7, 10). So we read in Matthew 28:16, "Then the eleven disciples went to Galilee, *to the mountain* where Jesus had told them to go" (emphasis mine). What mountain did Jesus have in mind?

In this chapter, we will consider the evidence and see that our final walk with Jesus takes us to the summit of Mount Arbel, on the west shore of the Sea of Galilee. Here we will see how Jesus used the view from the summit to present the scope of the work envisioned by the Great Commission. But we will also see that Mount Arbel is the most likely location for Jesus's Sermon on the Mount. When we link these two stories geographically, inquiring about their contribution to our mission, we will see that they join to define both what we should say and to whom we should say it.

Let's start with the Great Commission, the words that close the gospel of Matthew (28:16–20). They deserve our attention because they are the final words that Jesus spoke in Galilee, as well as the final words we hear from Jesus in Matthew's book.

Jesus begins by certifying his authority: "All authority in heaven and on earth has been given to me" (Matthew 28:18). This is a necessary step, since within first-century Judaism, religious teachers are "authorized" to teach by someone else who has been authorized. This typically happened within the confines of the rabbinic school system centered in Jerusalem, and it explains why the chief priests and elders repeatedly challenged Jesus with questions like, "By what authority are you doing these things? . . . And who gave you this authority?" (Matthew 21:23).

While he was in Jerusalem, Jesus did not answer these questions. But here in Galilee, as he authorizes the disciples to teach, Jesus declares that his authority exceeds that of anyone else. It is that authorizing power that lies behind the mission.

Now Jesus changes both the content and the scope of the disciples' teaching. Earlier, Jesus had focused his own teaching on the arrival and the nature of the heavenly kingdom (Matthew 4:23; 13:1–52). He had sent out the disciples to deliver this simple message: "The kingdom of heaven has come near" (Matthew 10:7).

Though the disciples were anxious to tell people more about their experiences with Jesus, he limited the content of what they could share (Matthew 12:16; 16:20). But now, in Galilee, the restriction is removed. The disciples are told to teach about *everything* they have seen and heard.

Jesus also expanded the scope of their work. At first, Jesus had directed his followers to speak only with the descendants of Abraham. "Do not go among the Gentiles or enter any town of the Samaritans," he had said. "Go rather to the lost sheep of Israel" (Matthew 10:5–6). The Great Commission completely removes those limitations: "Therefore go and make disciples of all nations" (Matthew 28:19).

But what mountain was the setting for this Great Commission? Matthew tells us of a specific mountain, but he does not use a proper name. This is not unusual, as he wrote the Greek word for "mountain" sixteen times but identified only one mountain by name—the Mount of Olives (Matthew 21:1; 24:3; 26:30). In all other cases, we need to use clues that Matthew provides to determine which mountain he has in view.

We discussed this in the previous chapter. On two occasions, Matthew described the setting as a "high mountain" (4:8; 17:1). That language allowed us to identify the setting for Jesus's first temptation—as well as the temptation that came from the mouth of Peter—as Mount Hermon. So what clues does Matthew offer that might help us identify the mountain on which Jesus gave the Great Commission?

First, this is a mountain that stands out from all others. "Then the eleven disciples went to Galilee, to the mountain where Jesus had told them to go" (Matthew 28:16). We know that Jesus had favorite places to teach (John 18:2), and in this case he seems to direct the disciples to meet him on a prominent mountain in Galilee he had used before.

Second, we know that Jesus often incorporated the view from the teaching location into his lesson. We have seen this repeatedly in the stories we have discussed. That leads us to look for a mountain that would fit the *theme* of the Great Commission—that is, a mountain whose view supports the transition in the message the disciples are to share and the people with whom they should share.

I believe that the best candidate is Mount Arbel. It is the most prominent mountain on the Sea of Galilee shoreline, rising 1,245 feet above the lake. It offers a view that takes in both the limited scope of the disciples' initial mission at its base, and the more distant reach to the nations.

As soon as I correlate this event with this place, a wave of geographic déjà vu sweeps over me. I have been here before. This is the same setting Jesus had used to deliver the Sermon on the Mount (Matthew 5–7), one of the longest and most detailed lessons Jesus taught. It probes the complex corners of the human experience, informing members of his kingdom how they may best think and live.

Let's consider the evidence that allows us to identify Mount Arbel as the setting for the Sermon on the Mount. First, Matthew indicates that we are on a specific mountain, using the Greek definite article in both 5:1 and 8:1 to indicate he is referring to a particular location, "the mountain." When we add the language of Matthew 4:23 and 8:5, we see that that this mountain is in Galilee, near Capernaum.

Second, the mountain must be tall enough and challenging enough to discourage crowds from following Jesus to the place where he's teaching. The Sermon on the Mount was advanced instruction meant first for the disciples (5:1). It was very hard for Jesus to find the isolation he sought where the terrain was easy. But by climbing a mountain like Mount Arbel, he could achieve the privacy he wanted for this intimate time of teaching.

Third, Mount Arbel solves the apparent contradiction between Matthew and Luke as they describe the setting for the Sermon on the Mount. Matthew says it took place "on a mountainside" (5:1) while Luke describes it as a "level place" or plain (6:17). Mount Arbel is both. From the north and east, it presents as a dramatic mountain cliff, the most striking physical rock face along the Sea of Galilee shoreline. But when you stand on top of the mountain, or view it from the south or west, you see a gently sloping plateau.

Fourth, the view from the summit of Mount Arbel provides a view that supports and enhances the content of Jesus's lessons. For example, the Sermon on the Mount begins with the beatitudes (5:3–10). These cherished verses survey life as God sees it rather than how people on earth might. The great majority of people in Galilee were living at or below subsistence levels, so it was hard for them to reconcile their circumstances with the words of Psalm 1, celebrating how blessed believers are. From the top of Mount Arbel, Jesus invited the disciples to get a view from the heavenly Father's perspective.

Members of the Lord's kingdom are rich, even though they feel poor. They will find comfort beyond their grief. They will inherit the earth, even if they feel trodden down into it. As Jesus taught this lesson from the summit, he did not ask the disciples to imagine people like that—from the viewing platform of Mount Arbel, he invited the disciples to observe the lives of the people below, people who did not feel blessed. From this high perch, Jesus told the disciples to think of these people as his Father saw them—blessed in every way, despite circumstances that suggested otherwise.

Mount Arbel also accounts for the two metaphors Jesus uses right after the beatitudes. First, he said in Matthew 5:13, "You are the salt of the earth." At the base of Mount Arbel, the disciples could see Magdala, a little village where people purchased fish caught in the Sea of Galilee, then processed them for resale. To lengthen the shelf life of the fish, salt was applied. With Magdala in view, Jesus urged the disciples to be salt.

Then Jesus lifted the disciples' eyes to the eastern shore of the Sea of Galilee and said, "You are the light of the world. A town built on a hill cannot be hidden" (5:14). Looming over the eastern shoreline was Hippos, a Decapolis city built to convince people that the Greco-Roman religion and way of thinking were superior. To support this claim, a sprawling city was built on a prominent hill and lighted at night. Jesus urged the disciples to be this kind of cultural beacon, one that attracts others to the kingdom.

Adding up all the evidence, Mount Arbel is the most likely setting for the Sermon on the Mount. But why would Jesus bring the disciples back to this mountain in Galilee to give them the Great Commission?

First, Mount Arbel allowed Jesus to speak more concisely. He could direct the disciples to go and make disciples by their teaching without having to review what they needed to teach. The message they should share was contained in their previous experience on this mountain—and in the view from the mountain.

Second, the view from the summit of Mount Arbel illustrated the change in the scope of the disciples' ministry. They had been working among the descendants of Abraham in the small confines of the lake basin. Now Jesus enlarged their view, from the basin to the world. Far below them, they could see representatives of the world on the International Highway. And lifting their eyes to the distant horizon, they could see where the kingdom needed to go.

The Great Commission fills in some things the Sermon on the Mount seems to be missing. Great speeches always start and end with powerful words. But while the Sermon starts with a flourish—

the words of the Beatitudes—the close of the address does not reach the same rhetorical pinnacle. And the Sermon doesn't define with whom we should share the message it contains. But these "shortcomings" are supplied when we return to Mount Arbel at the close of Jesus's ministry.

Here we get the powerful crescendo that concludes the Sermon on the Mount. Here the Great Commission defines the scope of our mission. With this view in sight, Jesus now says to us, "Therefore go and make disciples of all nations, baptizing them in the name of the Father and of the Son and of the Holy Spirit, and teaching them to obey everything I have commanded you. And surely I am with you always, to the very end of the age" (Matthew 28:19–20).

The view has not changed and neither has our mission.

In this chapter, we have walked back to four locations we had visited with Jesus: the Decapolis, Bethany, Mount Hermon, and Mount Arbel. In each case, the return visit advanced our understanding of a dimension of our mission.

In the Decapolis, we saw how powerful our story with Jesus can be, that it is the message we are to share. In Bethany, we saw two stories that teach us how to grow our faith so it can provide a powerful testimony. At Mount Hermon, we became better acquainted with the tactics Satan uses against us as we work to complete our mission. And at Mount Arbel we reviewed two stories that help define the content and the scope of our mission as followers of Jesus.

1. Which chapter in this section had the greatest impact on you? Why?

2. What story can you share with someone who has not met Jesus? What change have you seen in others when you've told your story?

3. What distractions in life keep you from listening to Jesus with undivided attention? In what practical ways can you strengthen your focus while reading and studying God's Word?

4. When have you seen Satan at work trying to defeat the Kingdom of God? What signs indicate that Satan is working to defeat your mission?

5. What challenges do you face in accomplishing the Great Commission? Are there any places or things—like the disciples' view from Mount Hermon—that helps you envision the Kingdom's expansion to the entire world?

6. How has this study of the Bible changed you?

Appendix

GOSPEL HARMONY AND LOCATION LIST

THE LOCATION FOR JESUS'S ACTIONS and teaching can be determined in a variety of ways. The gospel writers may tell us where an event is occurring or imply that a series of linked events belong in a certain location. In the cases where the Gospels do not mention the setting, either the content of what Jesus is teaching or later church tradition can be used to propose a location.

	MATTHEW	MARK	LUKE	JOHN	LOCATION
Birth and Early Years of Jesus					
Birth of John the Baptist foretold			1:5–25		Ein Kerem Temple in Jerusalem
Birth of Jesus foretold to Mary			1:26–38		Nazareth
Mary visits Elizabeth			1:39–56		Ein Kerem
Birth and early life of John the Baptist			1:57–80		Ein Kerem
Birth of Jesus foretold to Joseph	1:18–25				Nazareth
Birth and naming of Jesus			2:1–21		Bethlehem
Jesus presented before the Lord			2:22–40		Temple in Jerusalem
Visit of the Magi	2:1–12				Jerusalem Bethlehem

	MATTHEW	MARK	LUKE	JOHN	LOCATION
Flight of the holy family and their return to the Promised Land	2:13–23				Egypt Nazareth
Jesus pursues understanding			2:41–52		Temple in Jerusalem
John prepares the way	3:1–12	1:1–8	3:1–20	1:19–28	Wilderness of Judea Jordan River
Baptism and Early Ministry of Jesus					
Baptism of Jesus	3:13–17	1:9–11	3:21–22	1:29–34	Jordan River near Bethany beyond the Jordan
Temptations of Jesus					
• Wilderness	4:1–4	1:12–13	4:1–4		Wilderness of Judea
• Temple	4:5–7		4:9–13		Temple in Jerusalem
• Very high mountain	4:8–11		4:5–8		Mount Hermon
Selection of disciples				1:35–51	Jordan River near Bethany Beyond the Jordan Galilee
First miracle, changing water into wine				2:1–11	Cana of Galilee
Discussion with Nicodemus				3:1–21	Jerusalem
John the Baptist testifies about Jesus				3:22–36	Aenon
Jesus heals the son of a royal official				4:43–54	Cana of Galilee
Jesus heals a disabled man on the Sabbath				5:1–15	Bethesda pool in Jerusalem
Jesus authorized and affirmed by the Father				5:16–47	Jerusalem

	MATTHEW	MARK	LUKE	JOHN	LOCATION
Ministry in Galilee					
Change in base of operation	4:12–17				Nazareth Capernaum
Selection of the 12 disciples	4:18–22; 9:9–13	1:14–20; 2:13–17	5:1–11; 5:27–32		Capernaum area
Teaching and healing in Capernaum	8:14–17	1:21–34	4:31–41		Capernaum
Ministry in the synagogues of Galilee	4:23–25	1:35–39; 3:7–12	4:42–44		Galilee
Sermon on the Mount	5:1–7:29	3:13–19	6:12–49; 11:1–13; 12:22–34		Mount Arbel
Healing a man with leprosy	8:1–4	1:40–45	5:12–16		Capernaum area
Healing the centurion's servant	8:5–13		7:1–10		Capernaum
Cost of following Jesus	8:18–22		9:57–62		Capernaum area
Authority demonstrated in the healing of a paralyzed man	9:1–8	2:1–12	5:17–26		Capernaum
Question on fasting	9:14–17	2:18–22	5:33–39		Capernaum area
Raising of Jairus's daughter	9:18–26	5:21–43	8:40–56		Capernaum
Healing a disabled and demon-possessed man	9:27–34				Capernaum area
Sending out the 12 disciples	9:35–11:1	6:6–13	9:1–6		Galilee region
Jesus and John the Baptist	11:2–19		7:18–35		Capernaum area
Woe on unrepentant towns	11:20–24		10:13–15		Capernaum
Jesus is rest for the weary	11:25–30				Capernaum

	MATTHEW	MARK	LUKE	JOHN	LOCATION
Anointed by a sinful woman			7:36–50		Capernaum
Lord of the Sabbath	12:1–14	2:23–3:6	6:1–11		Capernaum area
The Servant in Isaiah 42	12:15–21				Galilee area
Jesus and Beelzebul	12:22–37	3:20–30	11:14–28		Galilee area
Sign of Jonah	12:38–45		11:29–32		Galilee area
Jesus's family defined	12:46–50	3:31–35	8:19–21		Galilee area
Parables of Jesus	13:1–52	4:1–34	8:1–18		Capernaum area
Rejection in Nazareth	13:53–58	6:1–6	4:14–30		Nazareth
Arrest and execution of John the Baptist	14:1–12	6:14–29	3:19–20		Machaerus
Feeding of the 5000	14:13–21	6:30–44	9:10–17	6:1–15	Bethsaida area
Walking on water and healing the sick	14:22–36	6:45–56		6:16–24	Sea of Galilee Capernaum
Bread of life and response				6:25–71	Capernaum
Lesson on ritual purity	15:1–20	7:1–23			Capernaum
Healing the blind man at Bethsaida		8:22–26			Bethsaida
Death announcement	17:22–23	9:30–32	9:43–45		Galilee area
Paying the Temple tax	17:24–27				Capernaum
Entry into and leadership within God's kingdom	18:1–9	9:33–37	9:46–48		Capernaum
Parable of the lost sheep	18:10–14				Capernaum
Lessons on forgiveness	18:15–35				Capernaum
Accept all who are for us		9:38–41	9:49–50		Capernaum
Managing and defeating sin		9:42–50			Capernaum

	MATTHEW	MARK	LUKE	JOHN	LOCATION
Ministry beyond Galilee					
Raising the widow's son at Nain			7:11–17		Nain
Discussion with a Samaritan woman				4:1–42	Sychar
Stilling the storm and healing demon-possessed in the Decapolis	8:23–34	4:35–5:20	8:22–39		Sea of Galilee Decapolis
Healing in Phoenicia	15:21–28	7:24–30			Region of Tyre and Sidon
Healing a deaf man and feeding of the 4000	15:29–39	7:31–8:13			Decapolis
Lesson taught by the feeding of the 4000 and 5000	16:1–12	8:14–21			Sea of Galilee
Peter's great confession	16:13–20	8:27–30	9:18–20		Caesarea Philippi area
Death announcement	16:21–28	8:31–9:1	9:21–27		Caesarea Philippi area
Transfiguration	17:1–13	9:2–13	9:28–36		Mount Hermon
Healing a demon-possessed boy	17:14–21	9:14–29	9:37–43		Caesarea Philippi area
Lesson on divorce	19:1–12	10:1–12			Perea
Children in the kingdom	19:13–15	10:13–16	18:15–17		Perea
Lesson on wealth and the kingdom	19:16–30	10:17–31	18:18–30		Perea
Parable of the workers in the vineyard	20:1–16				Perea
Death announcement	20:17–19	10:32–34	18:31–33		Perea
Mother's request for James and John	20:20–28	10:35–45			Perea

	MATTHEW	MARK	LUKE	JOHN	LOCATION
Ministry in Judea					
Attending the Feast of Tabernacles				7:1–52	Temple in Jerusalem
Woman caught in adultery				8:1–11	Temple in Jerusalem
Jesus affirms his identity				8:12–59	Jerusalem
Healing the visually impaired man at the Siloam pool				9:1–41	Jerusalem
Jesus the Good Shepherd				10:1–21	Jerusalem
Attending the Feast of Dedication				10:22–42	Jerusalem Temple
Parable of the Good Samaritan			10:25–37		Wilderness of Judea
Only one thing is needed			10:38–42		Bethany
Teaching on prayer			11:1–13		Jerusalem area
Lessons from the lamp			11:33–36		Judea
Warning the Jewish religious leaders			11:37–12:12		Judea
Parable of the rich fool			12:13–21		Judea
Division in place of peace			12:49–53		Judea
Interpreting the times			12:54–59		Judea
Parable of the fig tree			13:1–9		Jerusalem area
Healing a disabled woman on Sabbath			13:10–17		Jerusalem area
Parable of the great banquet			14:1–24		Jerusalem

	MATTHEW	MARK	LUKE	JOHN	LOCATION
En Route to Jerusalem					
Samaritan opposition			9:51–56		Northern Samaria
Sending out the 72			10:1–24		Perea
Roadside parables			13:18–21		Perea
Wide and narrow roads			13:22–30		Perea
Sorrow over Jerusalem			13:31–35		Perea
Cost of being a disciple			14:31–35		Perea
Parables about lost things			15:1–32		Perea
Parable of the shrewd manager and other brief lessons			16:1–18		Perea
Rich man and poor Lazarus			16:19–31		Perea
Raising of Lazarus and response				11:1–54	Bethany Jerusalem Ephraim
Ten healed of leprosy			17:11–19		Border between Samaria and Galilee
Parable of the persistent widow			18:1–8		Perea
Story of the Pharisee and the tax collector			18:9–14		Perea
Healing of blind Bartimaeus	20:29–34	10:46–52	18:35–43		Jericho
Conversations with Zacchaeus			19:1–10		Jericho
Parable of the 10 minas			19:11–27		Near Jerusalem

	MATTHEW	MARK	LUKE	JOHN	LOCATION
Final Days in Jerusalem					
Triumphal entry	21:1–11	11:1–11	19:28–44	12:12–19	Mount of Olives Bethphage
Cleansing the Temple markets	21:12–17	11:15–19	19:45–48	2:13–16	Temple
Lesson linked to the withered fig tree	21:18–22	11:12–14, 20–26			Mount of Olives
Authority questioned	21:23–27	11:27–33	20:1–8		Temple
Parable of the two sons	21:28–32				Temple
Parable of the tenants	21:33–46	12:1–12	20:9–19		Temple
Death announcement				12:20–36	Temple
Persistent unbelief in Jerusalem				12:37–50	Temple
Lessons on obedience and humility			14:1–14		House of a prominent Pharisee
Parable of the wedding banquet	22:1–14		14:15–24		House of a prominent Pharisee
Lesson on paying taxes to Caesar	22:15–22	12:13–17	20:20–26		Temple
Marriage and the resurrection	22:23–33	12:18–27	20:27–40		Temple
The greatest commandment	22:34–40	12:28–34			Temple
Jesus as the Son of God	22:41–46	12:35–37	20:41–44		Temple
Woes pronounced on Jewish leaders	23:1–39	12:38–40	20:45–47		Temple
The poor widow's gift		12:41–44	21:1–4		Temple
Lessons on the end of time	24:1–51	13:1–37	12:35–48 17:20–37 21:5–38		Mount of Olives

	MATTHEW	MARK	LUKE	JOHN	LOCATION
Parable of the ten virgins	25:1–13				Mount of Olives
Parable of the talents	25:14–30				Mount of Olives
Fate of the sheep and the goats	25:31–46				Mount of Olives
The plot to execute Jesus matures	26:1–5	14:1–2	22:1–2		Mount of Olives Temple
Jesus anointed by Mary	26:6–13	14:3–9		12:1–11	Bethany
Judas agrees to betray Jesus	26:14–16	14:10–11	22:3–6		Temple
Passover preparation	26:17–19	14:12–17	22:7–13		Upper Room
Jesus anticipates Judas's betrayal	26:20–25	14:18–21	22:21–23	13:18–30	Upper Room
Rank in God's kingdom			22:24–30		Upper Room
Jesus washes the disciples' feet				13:1–17	Upper Room
Passover becomes Lord's Supper	26:26–30	14:22–26	22:14–20		Upper Room
Jesus anticipates Peter's denial	26:31–35	14:27–31	22:31–38	13:31–38	Upper Room
Jesus comforts the disciples				14:1–16:33	Upper Room
Jesus prays for himself and the church				17:1–26	Upper Room
Struggle in prayer	26:36–46	14:32–42	22:39–46	18:1	Gethsemane
Jesus is arrested	26:47–56	14:43–52	22:47–53	18:2–12	Gethsemane
Jesus before the Sanhedrin	26:57–68	14:53–65	22:66–71	18:13–14, 19–24	Home of Caiaphas
Peter's denial	26:69–75	14:66–72	22:54–62	18:15–18, 25–27	Home of Caiaphas
Death of Judas	27:1–10				Field of Blood
Jesus before Pilate	27:11–26	15:1–15	23:1–25	18:28–19:16	Palace of Herod

	MATTHEW	MARK	LUKE	JOHN	LOCATION
Soldiers mock Jesus	27:27–31	15:16–20	22:63–65		Praetorium
Jesus is crucified	27:32–56	15:21–41	23:26–49	19:16–37	Calvary
Jesus is buried and the guard is set	27:57–66	15:42–47	23:50–56	19:38–42	Calvary
Jesus's Resurrection to the Ascension					
Resurrection of Jesus	28:1–15	16:1–8	24:1–12	20:1–10	Calvary
Jesus and Mary Magdalene		16:9–11		20:11–18	Calvary
Jesus with the Emmaus disciples		16:12–13	24:13–32		Road to Emmaus and Emmaus
Jesus appears to the ten			24:33–49	20:19–23	Upper Room
Jesus appears to the eleven		16:14		20:24–31	Upper Room
Recalling of the disciples and reinstating of Peter				21:1–25	Sea of Galilee
Great Commission	28:16–20	16:15–18			Mount Arbel
Jesus's ascension		16:19–20	24:50–53		Mount of Olives

Along the Road
VIDEO STUDY GUIDE

The following material is based on author John Beck's seven-part video study also entitled *Along the Road*, sold separately as a DVD. Filmed on location in and around Israel, the videos provide striking visuals for many of the locales discussed in the preceding chapters. Though the book and DVD stand alone, they may be combined for the greatest educational benefit. Each video episode outline will direct you to the related chapter in this book.

Episode 1: Bethlehem—Birthplace of Salvation

Episode 2: Into the Wilderness—Baptism and Temptation

Episode 3: To Mount Moreh—Raising a Widow's Son

Episode 4: Toward the Gihon Spring—The Coronation

Episode 5: To the Decapolis—Casting Out Demons

Episode 6: To Mount Hermon—Son of the Living God

Episode 7: To Mount Arbel—Sermon on the Mount and the
        Great Commission

—————————————— Episode 1 ——————————————

BETHLEHEM—BIRTHPLACE OF SALVATION

Additional Reading: *Along the Road* chapter 2, "Walking with Jesus from Nazareth to Bethlehem"

Scripture Connection: Ruth; 1 Samuel 16; Luke 2:1–14

PROLOGUE

Perhaps no story in the Bible is more known and loved than the account of the birth of Jesus. In the tiny town of Bethlehem, an ancient scriptural promise from the book of Micah was fulfilled as the Savior was born. But did you know that Bethlehem appears other times in the Old Testament? Dr. John Beck takes us to modern-day Bethlehem, "a very good place for us to see how Old Testament stories influence our understanding of stories from the life of Jesus." We will see how geography connects events that happened hundreds of years apart.

LOOKING BACK ON THE JOURNEY

Questions for consideration and discussion

1. In Deuteronomy 6:6–7, Moses wrote: "These commandments that I give you today are to be on your hearts. Impress them on your children. Talk about them when you sit at home and when you walk along the road." How does this admonition relate to Dr. Beck's study? What are some practical ways you can share God's truth with the people around you daily?

2. What do you think Dr. Beck means with his term "geographic déjà vu"? Can you think of any two Bible incidents, other than those he mentions in Episode 1, that happened in the same geographic location?

3. What does Dr. Beck identify as the two significant Old Testament stories that occur in Bethlehem? What is the key prophecy that mentions Bethlehem?

4. Dr. Beck says that Bethlehem stories are always about how the Lord comes to help people in need. How did God meet the needs of a family and a nation in the two Bethlehem stories of the Old Testament? How did He meet the needs of all humanity in the birth of Jesus?

5. The phrase "fear not" appears dozens of times in the Bible. Why would Dr. Beck say the "fear not" of Luke 2:10, spoken by angels to shepherds outside Bethlehem, is so important?

6. As you see how Scripture ties Ruth's story to David's to Jesus's—and connects them all via Bethlehem—what does this say to you about the Bible's trustworthiness? About God's story of redemption?

— Episode 2 —

INTO THE WILDERNESS—
BAPTISM AND TEMPTATION

Additional Reading: *Along the Road* chapter 8, "Walking with Jesus into the Wilderness"

Scripture Connection: Matthew 3:13–17; Matthew 4:1–4; Deuteronomy 8; Romans 7:15–20

PROLOGUE

Of all the things that happened to Jesus during his time on earth, perhaps the incident we can relate to most is his confrontation with the devil in the wilderness. We know about temptation—we all face it. And in the wilderness we discover that Jesus faced that same threat. In this episode, Dr. John Beck gives Jesus's temptation story a new dimension as he draws parallels to the wilderness experience of the Israelites under Moses.

LOOKING BACK ON THE JOURNEY

Questions for consideration and discussion

1. Though Jesus's wilderness experience did not occur in the same location as the Israelites', Dr. Beck points out that they happened in similar ecosystems. In what ways does the Lord's wilderness story parallel that of God's people under Moses? What, according to Dr. Beck, was the question God was asking both Jesus and the Israelites?

2. How did the experiences of Jesus and the Israelites ultimately, as Dr. Beck says, "diverge from each other"?

3. Dr. Beck points out that the place of Jesus's baptism was near the spot where the Israelites crossed into the Promised Land after their wilderness journey finally ended.

   What does Dr. Beck mean when he says that after the Israelites crossed the Jordan they began "their public ministry"? What changes did His baptism in the Jordan bring to Jesus's life?

4. One of the key teachings of this episode is Dr. Beck's explanation of why Jesus is so much more than just a "noble example to follow." How does Jesus rise above biblical figures such as Abraham, David, or Moses?

5. How well do you relate the apostle Paul's words in Romans 7:19 ("For I do not do the good I want to do, but the evil I do not want to do—this I keep on doing")? How does Jesus's successful experience in the wilderness help us? (See Philippians 3:8–9.)

6. How important to the Christian faith is it that Jesus was tested and tempted "in every way, just as we are—yet he did not sin" (Hebrews 4:15)?

—————————————— Episode 3 ——————————————

TO MOUNT MOREH—RAISING A WIDOW'S SON

Additional Reading: *Along the Road* chapter 14, "Walking with Jesus to Mount Moreh"

Scripture Connection: Matthew 2:23; Luke 7:11–17; 2 Kings 4:8–37

PROLOGUE

Jesus of Nazareth, they called him. Back in the day, Nazareth wasn't much to brag about. Maybe four acres in size, with perhaps eleven or twelve homes where Jesus's boyhood friends would have lived. It was a town geographically isolated from the influence of the pagan-Roman world. Once Jesus began his public ministry, most of his time was spent near Capernaum. But he returned to region of his boyhood home on several occasions. One of those trips took him to the village of Nain, near the base of Mount Moreh, just a few miles south of Nazareth.

LOOKING BACK ON THE JOURNEY

Questions for consideration and discussion

1. Why do you think God chose to have Jesus grow up in such a small, unimportant village as Nazareth?

2. Though Nazareth is mentioned several times in the New Testament—usually in the phrase "Jesus of Nazareth" —Dr. John Beck has noted that only one story is told about the town. Why would he say "it's not a very pretty story"? (See Luke 4:14–30.)

3. In the nearby village of Nain, Jesus had a very different reception. What did he do to cause the people to say "a great prophet has appeared among us" (Luke 7:16)? Can you think of other occasions when Jesus was identified as a prophet? (If you need help, see Matthew 21:11, John 4:19, and Mark 6:4.)

4. Dr. Beck goes to another town, located on the other side of Mount Moreh, for a related Old Testament story. What had happened in the nearby village of Shunem? (See 2 Kings 4:8–37.)

5. Are you surprised by the geographic proximity of Elisha's and Jesus's miracles? What do you think of Dr. Beck's contention that Jesus performed his miracle in this place to get a particular response from the people?

6. As you consider Dr. Beck's final words of this episode—"A great prophet has risen among us. God has mercy on his people"— think of some of the ways, both big and small, that you have experienced God's mercy through Jesus.

———————————— Episode 4 ————————————

TOWARD THE GIHON SPRING—
THE CORONATION

Additional Reading: *Along the Road* chapter 15, "Walking with Jesus toward the Gihon Spring"

Scripture Connection: Matthew 21:1–11; Mark 11:1–10; Luke 19:29–44; John 12:12–19; 1 Kings 1:28–35

PROLOGUE

Entering Jerusalem was nothing new for Jesus; he had done this many times during his life and ministry. But on the day we now call Palm Sunday, things were different. And one of the key differences was that this time he was greeted by adoring crowds. Dr. John Beck explains the geographic backstory that contributes to this celebratory entry into the City of David.

LOOKING BACK ON THE JOURNEY

Questions for consideration and discussion

1. What do you recall about the original Palm Sunday? What people, places, and things were involved in Jesus's "triumphal entry" into Jerusalem?

2. In this episode, Dr. John Beck notes, "Jesus could have simply said, 'I am the king, the son of David who will be the Messiah.' There's great power in that. But I think it's even more powerful when Jesus enacts an event that leads others to draw that

conclusion." What does he say Jesus enacted from the prophecy of Isaiah 40:1–5?

3. What other Old Testament prophecy, from Zechariah 9:9, did Jesus enact on Palm Sunday? What does Dr. Beck say the Passover pilgrims understood when they "put together all of those Mount of Olives stories"?

4. In what ways did Jesus's entry into Jerusalem parallel Solomon's from a thousand years earlier? What did the people around Jesus shout in response? How does Dr. Beck describe their language?

5. Imagine being among the crowds that waved palm branches as Jesus passed by. You know the of prophecy, perhaps, so you are expecting a king. As you watch, what kind of king are you anticipating?

6. Dr. Beck explains the meaning of Jesus as King in our lives— that he protects us and gives our lives meaningful direction. How have these two realities been manifested in your life?

──────────────── Episode 5 ────────────────

TO THE DECAPOLIS—
CASTING OUT DEMONS

Additional Reading: *Along the Road* chapter 17, "Walking with Jesus to the Decapolis"

Scripture Connection: Mark 5:1–20; Luke 8:26–39; Mark 7:31–37; 8:1–21

PROLOGUE

Mostly located east of the Jordan River, the ten cities of the Decapolis contrasted greatly with the Jewish communities to their west. Culturally, the Decapolis was Greco-Roman and religiously, it was pagan. Yet there was Jesus, the Jewish rabbi, hanging out on what seemed to be the wrong side of the lake—twice. In this case, we are not revisiting a place we've read about in the Old Testament; we are coming back to a place that Jesus himself has been before. And we wonder, as Dr. John Beck asks in this episode, "What's he doing over here?"

LOOKING BACK ON THE JOURNEY

Questions for consideration and discussion

1. What does it say about Jesus that he made the effort to leave the familiarity of Jewish territories to visit the Decapolis, which was decidedly Gentile?

2. The demon possession Dr. Beck describes from Mark 5 is horrible. The man in the story was so dangerous that he had been put in chains and forced to live in a graveyard. When Jesus and the disciples arrived by boat from Galilee, the man said, "What do you want with me, Jesus?" Why did he respond that way instead of asking for help?

3. Are you surprised that the people of this region would ask Jesus to leave immediately after he healed the demon-possessed man? Imagine someone showing up in your area and within minutes destroying your livelihood—that, it seemed, was what Jesus did when he sent the demons into these people's pigs. How reasonable is the residents' reaction?

4. Why was the healed man's request to follow Jesus back to Galilee denied? (See Mark 5:19.) How do we know that the man did what Jesus told him to do? (See Mark 8:1–10.)

5. Dr. Beck asks, "Why didn't Jesus allow [the man] to get in the boat and go back with him to a side of the lake that would allow him to grow more in his faith?" What can we learn about spiritual growth from this man's obedience?

6. Consider Dr. Beck's final observation: Jesus treated Gentiles who were hungry the same way he treated observant Jews who were hungry. He fed them both. What does that say about how we should treat people who might be on the other side of some political or religious or cultural line we have drawn?

— Episode 6 —

TO MOUNT HERMON—
SON OF THE LIVING GOD

Additional Reading: *Along the Road* chapter 19, "Walking with Jesus to Mount Hermon"

Scripture Connection: 1 Kings 12:25–30; Matthew 16:13–20; Mark 8:27–9:1

PROLOGUE

Dan was a city in the far north of Israel. In Old Testament times, it was a pagan worship center built by Jeroboam, first ruler of the ten northern tribes when the Jewish kingdom split after the death of Solomon. A nearby town called Caesarea Philippi was similarly noted for its pagan worship. So it might seem surprising that the antithesis to paganism—Jesus Christ—would come to this area to teach about who he really was: the Son of the living God.

LOOKING BACK ON THE JOURNEY

Questions for consideration and discussion

1. The beauty that Dr. John Beck enjoys in this region—rushing waters, singing birds, lush vegetation—contrasts with the darkness of its pagan history. Where do we see this contrast in our world, where light shines despite the darkness of unbelief?

2. Why would a Jewish ruler, Jeroboam, introduce elements of pagan worship into his own kingdom at Dan? (See 1 Kings

12:25–30.) Why might Christians today be tempted to incorporate worldly beliefs and practices into their faith?

3. At nearby Caesarea Philippi, Jesus asked the disciples, "Who do people say the Son of Man is?" What names did the disciples give? (See Matthew 16:13–14.) Why might the answers have differed here from in Galilee?

4. What was Jesus's next question to the disciples? What was Peter's answer? (See Matthew 16:16.)

5. Consider Jesus, standing before what many thought to be the gates of Hades, hearing the apostle Peter correctly answering the important question of "who the Son of Man is." How does this visual help us understand Jesus's response to Peter? How does Dr. Beck connect Matthew 16:17–18 to the geography of Caesarea Philippi?

6. What does Dr. Beck say was Jesus's primary purpose for visiting Caesarea Philippi? How does this journey—with Jesus and with Dr. Beck—encourage your faith?

—————————— Episode 7 ——————————

TO MOUNT ARBEL—SERMON ON THE MOUNT AND THE GREAT COMMISSION

Additional Reading: *Along the Road* chapter 20, "Walking with Jesus to Mount Arbel"

Scripture Connection: Matthew 5–7; Matthew 28:16–20

PROLOGUE

If you look for the name "Mount Arbel" in the Bible, you won't find it. Yet Dr. John Beck has identified this prominent mountain overlooking the Sea of Galilee as the best candidate for the location of both Jesus's Sermon on the Mount and his pronouncement of the Great Commission. You can read details about his contentions regarding Mount Arbel in chapter 20.

LOOKING BACK ON THE JOURNEY

Questions for consideration and discussion

1. As Dr. Beck started his ascent of Mount Arbel, he asked, "Are you up for a little bit of an adventure?" Is backpacking up a mountain—or just backpacking in general—something you would look forward to? What do you think the disciples may have been thinking as Jesus led them up the steep hillside?

2. Think about the powerful beginning of the Sermon on the Mount—the Beatitudes. What effect might the dramatic setting have had on the disciples' hearing of Jesus's teaching?

3. What do you think of Dr. Beck's suggestion that the majestic opening lines of the Beatitudes (Matthew 5:3–12) are not matched by an equally powerful close to the discourse (Matthew 7:25–34) . . . that "the last paragraph of the Sermon on the Mount" is instead the Great Commission as recorded in Matthew 28?

4. How did Jesus change the "scope of the disciples' ministry . . . on top of Mount Arbel"? (See Matthew 28:19.) Have you ever thought of how important the Great Commission is to you personally—as it was with Dr. Beck through his forebears in Europe?

5. What an evocative thought from the top of Mount Arbel: "This view hasn't changed since the disciples heard [the Great Commission]. And neither has our mission." How does this speak to your heart? What changes might you make in life after hearing this challenge?

6. Which of the seven geographical connections in this series by Dr. Beck has been most surprising to you? How has his teaching affected the way you view God's Word?

Enjoy this book? Help us get the word out!

Share a link to the book or
mention it on social media

Write a review on your blog, on a retailer site,
or on our website (dhp.org)

Pick up another copy to share with someone

Recommend this book for your
church, book club, or small group

Follow Discovery House on
social media and join the discussion

Contact us to share your thoughts:

 @discoveryhouse    @DiscoveryHouse

Discovery House
P.O. Box 3566
Grand Rapids, MI 49501 USA

Phone: 1-800-653-8333
Email: books@dhp.org
Web: dhp.org